GOD'S PROMISES

God's Promises

A Journal of Personal Growth & Discovery

SHIRLEY LUNDY-CONNOR

BLESSED ASSURANCES PUBLISHERS LLC
NEW ORLEANS, LOUISIANA

Publisher's Note

This book, *God's Promises*, is designed to provide information in regard to the subject matter covered-(Spiritual. Self-Help. Christian. Recovery.). It is sold with the understanding that the publisher and author are not engaged in rendering formal psychiatric, psychological, legal, medical, or financial advice. If expert formal—(Spiritual. Self-Help. Christian. Recovery) assistance is required the services of a competent professional should be sought.

The purpose of this book, *God's Promises*, is to educate, motivate, encourage and inspire. With healing for the reader being the ultimate outcome. The author and Blessed Assurances Publishers LLC shall have neither liability nor responsibility to any person or entity with respect to any loss or damage caused, or alleged to be caused, directly or indirectly, by information contained in this book. The author and publisher want you, the reader, to heal. Be vigilant regarding your mental, emotional, and physical health. And if at anytime (during this process of personal growth and discovery and healing) there comes a time when additional support from a professional is needed, immediately seek out the counsel of a qualified professional.

Unless otherwise stipulated, all Bible quotes, Thomas Nelson Publishing Company, Nashville—New York.

First Edition

Publisher:
Blessed Assurances Publishers LLC
P.O. Box 870306
New Orleans, Louisiana 70187-0306

Editor: Barbara Winslow Robidoux. Ebword@aol.com
Cover Design: Shirley Lundy-Connor. Paul Dauphin.
Photograph by Shirley Lundy-Connor
Sunrise on Haleakala, (Maui Hawaii) 1998

Publisher's Cataloging-in-Publication
(Provided by Quality Books, Inc.)

Lundy-Connor, Shirley.
   God's promises : a journal of personal growth &
discovery / Shirley Lundy-Connor. — 1st ed.
   p. cm.
   LCCN 2004097285
   ISBN 0-9677089-1-5

   1. Spiritual life—Christianity. 2. God—
Knowableness. 3. Spiritual formation.   I. Title.

BV4501.3.L86 2005   248.4
                           QBI05-700011

DEDICATION

To Silas Connor
My Best-Friend
My Partner In Life
My Husband

You have shown
Solid and fixed faith in me.
You have put
cupped-hands beneath me
And said —
Soar
Soar high as you like.
I'll spot you
I'll spot you for safety.

ACKNOWLEDGEMENTS

To every man, woman, and child who has walked the grace journey —
Life — I thank you. Your courage has inspired me. From your example I
learned there was *Life* after death. I learned that one of God's Promises is
Life everlasting.

I have sat with the rape victim, the incest survivor, the confessed and
contrite murderer, the parents and relatives and friends of the murdered,
the battered and abused spouse, the batterer, the child who could not read
as well as desired and expected, the unwed mother, the welfare mother
and father, the aged man, the aged woman, the physically sick and
infirmed, *you* whom society in essence threw away — and, I saw grace...
God's grace. Thank you. A sentence of death, walking death, had been
administered to each of you. And, you, each of you, in defiance of that
death-sentence rose — Phoenix that you are — from the ashes. Your bravery
is interspersed throughout these pages.

I value and respect your privacy. And so, therefore, names have been
changed. Specific incidents have been merged and composites of various
situations created.

You were my first teachers, prompting me to seek out my other
teachers. My other teachers have been varied and copious. You, as *other*
teacher, have taken on many forms. Books. Lectures. Tapes. Observations.
And so, therefore, nothing set down herein is presented as original. Of the
hundreds, thousands, of *other* teachers, those resources (people, books,
theories, etc.) that have become an integral part of my therapeutic practice,
I have cited. To the best of my ability I have correctly quoted theory and

concept—the essence of the theory. I apologize for any misquotes or failures to give proper citation. It is simply an offshoot of a dynamic of something my sixth grade teacher told me long ago: "Shirley when you can rephrase a sentence into your own words it is then that you have truly mastered the concept."

To all my teachers, I thank you for adding to my body of expertise, for adding to that which I have mastered. No matter how minute, every one of the persons I have endeavored to lend aid, support, and assistance to has been truly helped through your work.

Special Acknowledgements

To:

All those who had and continue to have faith in me and what God is doing through me—*My Purpose* in life.

My editorial consultant, Barbara Winslow Robidoux. Without you I could not have done it.

Glenna Salsbury, National Speakers Association. I kept your note to me pasted on the wall, as inspiration to keep going, for five years! You said, and I quote: "My how the Lord has blessed you with the ability to communicate with meaning, emotion and grand picture words."

Tracie Thevenote. How does one say thank you for a life. You have been my beacon of light through many dark tunnels. We discovered my gifts, together.

Alvart Badalian. Arrow Graphics, Inc.

My Litany-of-Saints

Silas Connor, my partner-in-life, best friend and husband; our children—those born flesh-of-our-flesh as well as those who grew in the heart; our grandchildren, sisters, brothers, friends, and relatives.

"K"—Karen Sidney-Reine. My daughter who continuously called me and said: "You can do it. You doing it, Ma! You doing it!"

My son, Mark J. Sidney. Our Journey together began when I was 16-years old. The unconditional love that I was able to experience & express on that day led to a lifetime of hope-laden service.

My birth-mom, Miss Lucy, Luberta Gauldon. Look what reading to your baby while she was in the womb brought forth! Thanks! Lucy.

My birth-father, Walter Gauldon. Amen! What's in your heart-of-heart tells the story.

Two women to whom I was literally brought to (at birth) from the hospital. My other moms—Aunt Dorothy, Dorothy Williams, and Auntie Elon, Elon Meadows.

My "moms" at church: Miss Mae (Walker). Mrs. Sylvester (Miss Velma). Mrs. Laura Pieno. Mrs. Gloria Armand. Mrs. Dorothy Williams. Mrs. Mamie Palermo. Mrs. Cecile LaSalle. Words can not express how much your smiles, those looks of love in your eyes as you have gazed upon me, and warm embraces have meant to me.

My emotional father Uncle Charles, Charles Meadows. Thank you for literally always being there for me since birth.

Joyce Zonana. To whom many years ago I brought rough-rough written messages from the heart and you said, "Write. You have talent, write!"

Monica Pierre, Paul Dauphin, Cathy Harris & "Ray." And all of you from the Maui Writers Retreat—(Sam Horn, Tad Bartimus, Dan Poyntner, Bud Gardner, Ernest J. Gaines, Terry McMillan, Jack Canfield, Bryce Courtenay, and Elizabeth Pomada) who let me know: *No matter what else you do when you go home, you are a writer! And you must write.* And then there is: Rev. Douglas Doussan. Sharon Carter Sheridan. Barbara Williams. Rita Williams. Audrey Washington. Adrell Lawrence Pinkney. St. Joseph The Worker Adult Gospel Choir, Mr. Clark Knighten Music Minister. Pastor Paul McQuillen. Joyce Taylor.

Each of you (in my Litany-of-Saints), in some way, have cheered me on, had faith in me, and helped me in some way to get *God's Promises* into the hands of the reader.

CONTENTS

CHAPTER 1

"Oh my God!" moments in life • Life events that shake the very foundation upon which we stand • Death • Gut- wrenching occurrences that make us step back & recoil in disbelief • Having to (involuntarily) let go of someone or something • Feel like we are carrying around a permanent load of bricks • Losses—the idea, the hope, that all will be well; that all will remain the same, that *"that person will always be here."*

God's Promise: I will always be with you — no matter how bad it seems.

CHAPTER 2

Years of sacrifice—time, money, wants, needs • We *forget* about us • We forget that there is a self • We put self aside • We get caught up in taking care of others • We get bogged down in trying to make it happen/trying to force solutions • Excruciating disappointments • Self-imposed hells.

God's Promise: Peace and Serenity.

CHAPTER 3

Times of confusion • Situations that keep you shaking your head • Situations, that for the life of you, you just can't make sense out of • Betrayal • Spirits low: Lord are You listening? Can You hear me? Where are You, Lord? Why haven't you fixed this? • *When* are you going to fix this/them? • Pray for help. Help seems out of reach and not forthcoming • Turn problem over to God; God not working fast enough • Snatch it back.

God's Promise: I will make sense out of no sense.

"Do not be afraid or discouraged. I your Lord am the one who goes before you. I will neither fail you nor forsake you" (Dt. 31:8).

CHAPTER 4

Change—continuous and insidious • Illness • The only constant is change • We are forever in a struggle with the process of change • Sudden, life-shattering occurrences that shake us to our very core • Pain • Shock • Suffering • Grave news • Catastrophe • The unending struggle with the process of change.

God's Promise: I will be your doctor in times of sickness.
Each and every experience that you go through I'll be in the midst of it.
I will heal you both physically and spiritually.

"...for I am the LORD that healeth thee. And they came to Elim, where were twelve wells of water, and threescore and ten palm trees: and they encamped there by the waters" (Exodus 15:23KJV).

"For I will restore health to you. And heal you of your wounds" (Jeremiah 30:17)

CHAPTER 5

Old wounds—spiritual and emotional • Injurious afflictions • past abuse—verbal, emotional, physical, sexual • untreated sickness • hidden wounds • Type A personalities • impatient; quick-tempered • inertia • listlessness • broken legs • broken hearts • broken spirits • depression • weight problems • eating disorders • compulsive overeating • bulimia • anorexia • drug/alcohol problems.

God's Promise: I will fortify and strengthen you;
I will heal you of all that has hurt you.
I will be that shoulder for you to cry on.
I will be the Eternal Arms that encircle you and hug you.

"And, Jesus told him: Stand up! Pick up your mat, and go home ...You are healed" (Mark 2:11 LTB)

CHAPTER 6

Patterns of behavior • Learned behaviors • Imitated behaviors • Abused becomes the abuser • Soul-murderers • Wounded, wound • Hidden mindsets • Hidden hurts • Hidden guilts • Hidden shame • Hidden grief • Rhyme, rhythm—social order.

God's Promise: I will teach you a new way.
I shall open up the gates of love for you.
I will hold you up in times of weakness. I will be your real teacher.
I will be the gentle cool wind to soothe your heated brow when you are troubled.
I will be the Eternal Arms that encircle you and hug you.
I will be the love that fills your heart and mind and soul and spirit and hand—
as you lift your hand to touch another.

CHAPTER 7

.

INTRODUCTION

GOD'S PROMISES. What a profound statement. Does God need to promise us anything?

I think not.

Healing. Joy. Hope. Abundance. Laughter. Calmness. Serenity. Blessings. Sought after commodities by both men and women.

And, it is in the seeking of these things, quite extraordinarily, that a great deal of chaos is realized.

There is something each living human being has in common. A heartbeat. Even, if it is through some artificial means. And within each heartbeat, the actual motor by which it runs is God: *The Spirit-of-God.* Eternal. Everlasting. Pulsating with: Power. Hope. Joy. Laughter. Promise. Cures. Restoration. Peace.

In *God's Promises* you will find the hope and the promise of each heartbeat.

Certain chapters, just through the necessity of giving you more detailed instruction on how to walk through the exercises, are longer than others. Some, are shorter, needing less instruction. Whether long or short *each* contains detailed instruction on how to heal. Each chapter has activities (*Activities of Prayer*) for you to complete that are designed for your healing.

Philosophers, deep introspective thinkers, Spiritual women, theologians, healers of all kind, tell us that healing entails a fundamental action on our part. And that is to embrace the moment—to grab hold of and bring into our hearts, Now. Now, *this* moment, is always filled with God. Where God is, is a healing.

My passion and strength, indeed what I have found to be *my purpose*, is to reinforce, daily, in that which I think, say, and do, (and thereby give instruction to others, hopefully, through example), the following: That God *Is*. That God can and will, if sought. That all pain has a beginning and an end. That instruction, although sometimes painful, is just that, a lesson- -not punishment, as I, for many years, thought it to be. That one breath, literally, contains all that I seek—solution, health, God.

Through the writing of *God's Promises*, I have endeavored, to share these truths with you.

In this book, you will find my heart, healed now, from years of being cracked open by a sledgehammer of pain. It was laid bare by trauma. It was wounded by deceit.

I dragged along this hurt, unknowingly, for decades. And then, through the grace of God "I picked up a book." In it the author said: "Has anyone so violated your boundaries that it defied rational thought? Could you have been so profoundly hurt that you have blocked it out of your conscious mind? Is there some unknown fear that seems to haunt you, cropping up every now and then?"

In my scariest inner-voice I had to answer yes. And with that came the beginning of the rest of my life.

Pain—witnessed and experienced, once healed, is even more validated by the using of it to reach out and help someone else.

That, is the intention of *God's Promises*. To use the pain once felt and now healed from as well as my clinical skills honed through the many years of extending professional help to both children and adults to offer assistance to you.

And so, I ask: What are *you* faced with, on today? Did someone die? Have you ever been betrayed? Are you, your child, husband or wife, relative or friend drinking too much, or abusing drugs? Have you or someone you care about been diagnosed with a serious illness? Did you feel as though someone kicked you in the gut on September 11th, 2001 and *your* world exploded? Were you hurt as a child? Has your anger or behavior ever been such or ever gotten out of control to the point that it scared you?

If you answered yes to any of these questions, or think perhaps you could have answered yes, then *God's Promises* is for you.

Within its pages you will find gentle and loving instruction on how to heal from these hurts.

And if the hurt is hidden, you will be coached on ways to uncover (in a safe, assisted manner) "the hidden": hidden hurts; hidden mindsets; hidden past abuses; hidden fears; hidden regrets; hidden guilt; hidden hate; and hidden rage.

Once the "hidden" is tapped into, you are then guided through a series of healing prayers, activities, affirmations, and suggestions on healing. All, designed to show you one thing—how to access and hold dear God's love.

But before we begin I want to share with you one of the fundamental ways in which I have found to assist one to globally heal; to heal spiritually, emotionally, mentally and physically. It is a form of prayer. A *prayer as close as the next breath you take*. And, it is called breathing.

In order to engage in breathing as an activity of prayer, it is important that you quiet yourself, that you stop, and be still, for a moment.

Next, let a smile gently find its way to your lips. Slightly part your lips. With this smile on your face breathe in deeply through your nose. Breathe in wholly. Allow your chest and tummy to fully extend up and out. Then, release the collected air through the small opening in your lips. Good. Take another deep cleansing breath, making sure you fill both your lungs and tummy. Hold that breath to the count of 1...2...3. And from the hole created from your slightly parted lips slowly let go and gently release the collected air.

Let's try that again. Take a deep breath; fill your lungs as far as possible. Your chest should expand and your tummy should extend outward if you are breathing in correctly. Good. Feel your tummy extend as the air(God) flows into your body. With full and deliberate prayer(action) release all of the collected air. Relax. Untense those muscles. Let go.

Congratulations. You have just practiced taking the first of the many cleansing breaths you will take as we, together, travel this journey of health and healing.

Remember—monitor your breathing, and make a commitment—to freely breathe throughout each and every activity in this book.

God Bless. Let's start our Journey.

ONE

A...Chapter

A...Promise

THERE comes a time in each of our lives when the news is so devastating we "just can't bear it." I think about the mother, the father, the grandmother, the aunt, all those close to the parents of an infant girl who died at birth. The doctors said the little girl's head had been crushed as it traveled through the birth canal.

I think about the young woman whose two and three year old daughters got in her bed one Saturday morning to play with daddy, as was their custom, and "daddy didn't wake up."

I think back about the grief counselor at one of the hospitals, who was riding home one night after work, and got a call on her cellular phone asking for the next of kin of her brother. And how she said that when hospital personnel took her into a room and the chaplain came in she *knew* her brother was dead. She would later say; "How many times had I done the same thing at the hospital where *I* worked; how many times had I taken a family into that ruthlessly, blindingly lit room and proceeded to fail royally at making the hearing of the news better?"

These life events shook the very foundations upon which these people stood. It is my thought that you, just by living, have also had situations occur in *your* life that have shaken the very ground that *you* have stood upon.

In this chapter we are going to explore how to get through those times when we feel like we are carrying around a permanent load of bricks—

when we appear to be saying: "Whew!" after such ordinary day to day activities as washing our face, brushing our teeth, or drinking a glass of water.

"Helen's Dead...Oh My God!"

I watched in astonishment as Miss Annie Green, a first generation descendant of slaves, told my grandmother, who shared that historical distinction with her, that her daughter had just suffered an aneurysm and died. We had called Miss Green out of desperation because none of us— not the eighteen-year-old me, my mother, nor my other living aunts— knew how to tell my granny we had just left the hospital where Aunt Helen had been pronounced dead.

It was my Mom who suggested we telephone Miss Green.

"She'll know what to say. She and Mama have been through so much during the years, Annie Green will know what to say."

And indeed she did.

"Lula, sit down. I've got some hard news for you. Helen died."

Lula Lundy's eyes narrowed as if squinting for understanding and then they appeared to dilate with full understanding.

"Oh my God!"

And then silence.

Eternal silence.

Most likely it was only a few seconds, but it *felt* like an eternity.

Tears glistened in Lula's eyes, at first defying gravity by just sitting there like two, too-full pools of water. And then they fell, raining on her cheeks, cleansing her neck and finally staining the bosom of her shirt with the evidence of grief.

"When did it happen? Where is she? What about Helen's children, Louise and them; do they know?"

And with that statement, as I had done so many times before, I watched her stand up; reach out for the hands of the person positioned in front of her; hold them slightly at arm's length; shake as though shaking off some rain that had gotten on her clothes during a spring drizzle; and, begin to pray.

I knew, this gesture, signaled, a call to action.

Lula Lundy was about to begin doing what she would later tell me was, the work of burial.

I'm sure being told your 41-year-old daughter, to whom you had spoken just a few hours earlier, was dead had to feel like one of the worst "Oh my God!" moments in life.

Wisdom gained from living tells me that most likely you too have had the type of gut wrenching occurrence that has made you step back, recoil, in disbelief.

Perhaps a death like my granny experienced.

Whatever it was, your experience entailed the letting go of someone or something.

When the loss is a someone, the grief most often is clear, evident. However, when the loss is a something that we have had to or will have to let go of, the grieving can be somewhat blurred.

Many times the something we grieve is the loss of the idea, the hope, that all will be well; that all will remain the same; that "that person will always be here."

According to grief experts, it is then that a condition, a state of being, called the grief process begins.

Some of these experts, such as Elisabeth Kubler-Ross M.D., say that the grief process has stages. These stages of grief have been identified as denial, anger, bargaining, depression (the stage most often cited as the cause of us feeling as though we are carrying around that permanent load of bricks), and the final stage, acceptance.

So how do we get from the stage of denial to the stage of acceptance, the stage these experts say is the door to healing? We take, a faith journey.

Imagine God holding your hand. Feels wonderful, doesn't it? With God holding your hand, let us together open up the door to grief. I want you to do this even if you don't think you have anything to grieve about, or even if you believe you have worked through the grief.

If you believe you have worked through the grief or have nothing to grieve about we can do something called "Let's pretend." In "let's pretend" we are going to act as if you have something to grieve about.

But before we begin, it is important that you quiet yourself, that you stop, and be still, for a moment. As you quiet yourself, breathe. As you have just learned how to do in the introduction. Breathe in wholly, tummy and chest fully extended. And then, let go. Release and let go the collected air. And if you are experiencing any type of low-grade fear or anxiety as you release the collected air simultaneously allow this uneasiness to go.

Remember—monitor your breathing, and make a commitment—to freely breathe throughout this, and each and every, activity in this book.

Now say out loud: **I know my God is here**. And with God holding your hand allow yourself to think back to when you got *your* "Oh my God!" news. Let yourself remember what happened that wheeled *you* around so fast, that you, as the earth does, whirled around at such a speed that you remained fixed, standing, in the place where you were—and you didn't know how that could possibly be.

Faith's Journey

Activity: Say the following:

I place my faith and trust in God. I want to trust that God's eternal goodness flows through the universe. I have been told that only goodness and mercy shall follow me all the days of my life. (Psalm 23:6 KJV) I have also been told that the heavens render up that which is sought. With that in mind, I commit to walking this journey. One, that I shall refer to as a journey of faith. With the hope, that all will be well.

Many times I have said: "It's okay; I'm all right; it's not that bad…it wasn't that bad." But it could very well be that I have been (or am) in denial. And so, today, as a sign of my willingness to live life more fully (no matter how frail that willingness is) I, to the best of my ability, give myself permission to remember those things that have happened in my life that have been painful and write them down, on the following lines.

Here is what happened to me.

_____

_____

_____

_____

_____

_____

_____

Now that you have an idea of what you could possibly be grieving over, let's talk about the way in which you might have been displaying that grief.

Have you been short tempered, annoyed, agitated, frustrated? Have you been trying to cope *all by yourself?*

The way Lula Lundy walked through that crisis over the loss of her daughter, sometimes crawling on her knees in *her walk,* was to call out for help. She called out for help and she let herself feel what she was feeling. I can remember her doing her chores, singing her hymns, and all the while talking out loud to God. "Lord, I know this is your will, but I sure don't like it!" It was then that she would be expressing her anger. It was then that she would be saying, "This is <u>not</u> okay with me!"

Continuing on with our journey of faith, let's pretend you have been mad about the loss or losses that have occurred in your life. Tell God what *you* are mad about. Tell God what *you* don't understand. While we are pretending, let's pretend you have been short-tempered and impatient with your mate, your children, your co-workers, whomever. Tell God how you have behaved with those people. Without blaming yourself or shaming yourself look back at your behavior and allow yourself to do the next activity.

Remember: God is with you!

Activity: Say (pray) the following

I place my faith, my hope, and my trust in *You,* Lord God Almighty. Continuing on with this faith journey, here is a description of how I have been behaving.

_____

_____

_____

_____

_____

You have trusted God, and loved yourself enough to list behaviors you have been displaying. Take a moment to pray again. Pray, and then look at the list. As you look at each behavior ask yourself two questions: Did this behavior bring me closer to God? Or, did this behavior separate me from God? I ask you to look at your behaviors without blame shame or critical judgment toward yourself. If you start being critical of yourself, you will stop the learning process. Instead of learning about *what* you have been doing to either connect to or separate from God, you will begin to feel sad, or ashamed, or afraid, or guilty. And when we start to feel, rather than think, we interrupt the learning process.

<u>Behavior Displayed</u>   **<u>Connected Me To/Separated Me From God?</u>**

_____   _____
                       (denial, anger, bargaining, acceptance)

_____   _____
                       (denial, anger, bargaining, acceptance)

_____   _____
                       (denial, anger, bargaining, acceptance)

_____   _____
                       (denial, anger, bargaining, acceptance)

Look at the list of behaviors you wrote down. As you look at each behavior determine, to the best of your ability, if you could have possibly been in a state of denial, anger, or bargaining with God (*Please don't let this happen! If you will just _____, I <u>promise</u> I will* (You fill in the blanks.) *Please don't let this be real!*). In addition to this, at various times, we could be in the preferred state of acceptance. Look closely at your behavior. Then, below each line, circle the level of grief that corresponds to that specific behavior.

Continuing on with our journey of faith, let us now determine how we can go about accepting (not liking) what has happened in our lives. When we accept what is happening in our lives, we stay present in the moment. When we fight with or struggle against what is occurring we engage in a tug-of-war with life circumstances. When we engage in these fits of will we separate ourselves from God. However, when we acknowledge what has happened, fall on our knees, scream out in anguish, and surrender, we empower ourselves to be in a continuous state of connectedness to God. And if we allow ourselves to think about it, in the final analysis this is really our only goal — to be one with God.

Continuing with this faith journey use the information you have become aware of to design a plan for health, healing, and acceptance. As defined in the 12 Step Programs acceptance is: "If God allows it, and I can't change it, then it must be the best thing for me and for those I love."

From my list I can tell that I have been mad about:

_____

_____

_____

_____

_____

I have raged about:

_____

_____

_____

_____

_____

I could have been in denial about:

_____

_____

_____

_____

_____

And, I notice I most probably have been bargaining with God about:

_____

_____

_____

_____

_____

I'm still standing but sometimes the load feels awfully heavy about:

_____

_____

_____

_____

_____

and, I just might be depressed about it.

Prayer

Dear God, I come to you in faith. Show me how to grieve. Show me how to express my anger over what has happened or what seems to be happening. Show me how to cry out in anguish, to scream, to holler, or to just sit with the pain. Show me how to release that person, that place, that thing, which I might be holding on to. Help me to remember that when I release and let go of *what was* I open wide a space for *You* to enter. And Lord, I ask that you help me to bear in mind that when I do this I have accepted (not liked) what has happened. And when I accept *Your Will* it is then, that I am, in a state of grace.

Affirmations

- God *is* the *Light* of my life.

- God *is* healing me.

- The pain of my grief has a beginning and an end.

- I am willing to feel this pain.

- God *is* in the midst of this grief.

- My tears will water my soul.

- God *is* healing me.

- I accept God's healing.

- God *is*…my light, my hope and my power.

- I am healed. I am healed. I am healed.

- The peace of God *flows* through every inch of my being; God's peace is a healing balm.

- I feel the grace of God; I feel the peace of God.
  (Repeat 3 times)

- I am healed. I am healed. I…am…healed!

Suggestions For Healing

Remember to Breathe

It has taken a tremendous amount of courage for you to begin this journey of faith. And, you are doing a great job! The very fact that you are on this page confirms this statement. In order to keep moving forward it is important that you do a few basic things. And the most needed practice for you to continue to observe is to breathe. We most often take breathing for granted because it is something we automatically do. We breathe, by and large, without any conscious thought about what we are doing. — *Living beings breathe*. However, breathing as a healing and cleansing form, as it is meant to be, is an art. As we begin this process and as you move along in the practice I want you to keep in mind a key point. Gentle and easy, *that* is how you are to experience this practice of breathing: in a very gentle and free of pain manner.

Let's begin. You can either sit in a comfortable position (feet flat on the floor, back positioned comfortably against a chair pillow or wall, forearms resting comfortably on your lap, hands facing up or down), or you can lie flat on your back on the floor or in bed, arms resting comfortably at your sides, palms up or down. Concentrate on your nose. Gently breathe in through your nostrils. Now release the air through your mouth.

One of the most comfortable ways in which to release the collected air in your lungs is to form a hole the size of a dime with your mouth. And then, gently let the air flow from this opening. Once again, concentrate on your nose. Breathe in through your nostrils. Breathe out through your mouth. Remember, from that dime size opening formed with your lips, slowly let it (*all the cares of the moment*) go.

Practicing breathing in this way, releasing the air bit by bit, has another benefit. It will keep you from being subjected to a sense of lightheadedness. This practice, following and being consciously aware of your breath, is referred to by Zen master Thich Nhat Hanh as mindfulness. We will discuss mindfulness later. Right now I want you to think about the way in which an infant lying on its back in a crib breathes in and out. Visualize how that baby's tummy goes up and down as it breathes in and out. As you practice, *this* is the way in which I want you to breathe.

Initially, repeat this process of breathing ten times. As you become more comfortable with this breathing process extend the time to 5, 10, 15, minutes. Your goal is to develop this breathing experience to the point that you will be able to observe 20-minute sessions at a time. And as you breathe in and out here are some suggested affirmations to say in your mind:

- *Breathing in, I embrace God.*

- *Breathing out, I <u>Let Go</u> fear.*

- *Breathing in, I fill my mind, my soul, my emotions, every cell in my body, with the love of God.*

- *Breathing out, I let go anxiety.*

- *Breathing in, I breathe in my Creator.*

- *Breathing out, I let go tension.*

- *Breathing in, I breathe in the power of God.*

- *Breathing out, I let go weakness.*

- *Breathing in, I breathe in Faith.*

- *Breathing out, I let go doubt.*

- *As I breathe in, the cells of my body are filled with the light of God.*

- *Breathing out I **release all stress.***

- *Breathing in I breathe in Blessed Assurance.*

- *Breathing out, I let go doubt and uncertainty*

- *Breathing in, I breathe in the Presence of God — And, keep it there*

Be Still

Say a prayer. Ask for your mind to be quieted so that your heart can be filled with the Presence of God. Sit still. Listen. If you allow yourself to be very still, you will actually be able to "watch your breath." This activity of following one's breath will nourish and cleanse every cell of your body as well as establish a sense of calmness within your emotions even during the most difficult of circumstances. By simply and gently listening to the rhythm of your breath you will be able to enter into a place of peace so beautifully described in Philippians 4 verse 7: *Then God's own peace, which is beyond all understanding, will stand guard over your hearts and minds, in Christ Jesus.* [NAB]

TWO

Another...Chapter
Another...Promise

❧

SOME of us get so caught up in what we are doing that we *forget* about us.

We forget that there is a self.

We move along at break-neck speed so intent on what we are trying to do that our focus, no matter what else we do, is remained fixed on a cherished outcome. And, God forbid, if what we are working on just happens to be "a real good thing"—we truly get caught up in, trying to *make it happen*!

Coming from a place of having "every good intention, in the world," we make sacrifices.

If, for example, we need a new dress, a new pair of shoes, or some new work clothes, we will put off buying the needed clothing so we can use the money for: *John. He really wanted...*

We sacrifice time, money, our wants, and many times our needs. "It's just for a little while. When I get—(*you fill in the blank*), then I'll buy those shoes, get that new dress, trade in the car, take that trip, make use of that vacation time that is owed me at work."

We put self aside. We reserve for another time that which we need and want. We do this so the desired outcome, most often an outcome associated with someone else, a dream we have for him or her, can become a reality.

15

What happens when the dream goes poof?

> *What happens*
> *when years of sacrifice*
> *goes fleetingly,*
> *as in a bird…*
> *Silently:*
> *Drifting.*
> *Lifting.*
> *up*
> *out, and off*
> *from the place where it was*
> *and,*
> *flies away…*
> *Up, up, up, and off,*
> *until we can no longer see it—*
> *as if it were never there,*
> *a dream,*
> *a distant memory,*
> *nowhere to be seen?*

Did it exist?

Was it all a dream?

In this chapter we will talk about renewal.

We shall discuss how to come back from Gahanna, the self-imposed hell, that yawning gulf of pain brought on by constant and insidious sacrifice on our part.

And as a means to heal we will talk about the value of self; how to claim self; and, the worthiness of self.

As we travel this journey of healing, we will discuss the plan; God's plan, for us.

We will walk through step-by-step instructions on how to access God: how to access God at will.

And, we shall also make clear, how once filled, once present, with God's Spirit—how to hold on, steadfast, to the Bosom of God.

"She What?...That Can't Be True!"

I have no idea how long I sat there, but the parking lot, which had been full (all 4000 square feet of it) was empty when I finally drove off in that old beat up Chevrolet.

As I sat there, a moving picture of that beloved girl's life screened before me. I could see her as infant, newly out of the womb, being placed on my chest, extending the bond of warmth known for a precious 9 months; and, as a two-day-old bundle being brought to me to be fed.

Had not this been what God had required of me all along? To feed her?

Had I not tried to feed her spiritually and mentally as well as physically?

Where had I gone wrong?

What had I done to cause her to cut school — as they said she had been doing; smoke pot — as they said she had been doing; mouth-off to teachers — as they said she had been doing; go to the liquor store during study-hall time — as *I* had witnessed her doing one cold (trails of smoke-like oxygen billowing out of your nose and mouth) December day in Chicago Illinois?

What, had I done wrong?

What, had I done to cause this child to go astray — as they said she had done?

I was in shock. From the time of her birth my reality, *that* upon which I made all decisions, had been my daughter and how each decision would affect her becoming the next great whatever.

When she was expelled, my world collapsed.

What does a mother or father do when that parent's dream for their child ends?

How does one find a way to go on?

On that day, I didn't know.

I had no answers.

Only — paralytic, unrecognized pain; concrete, blood drained from the extremities, 1965 Chevrolet burial chamber — stillness.

When the stark-cold reality of a dream deferred, a dream lost, hits you the experience is one of the most devastating moments in life.

Many times it can come upon you like a shock of ice-cold water being thrown in your face. At other times, it can take on a gauze-like quality, veiled and curtained in denial.

The denial, is aptly referred to by Claudia Jewett in her book, *Helping Children Cope With Separation and Loss*, as "the shock absorber of the soul."

Perhaps you, just by walking life's journey, have had the instant when you, if you could move, shook your head in total disbelief.

Was it a child, a husband, a wife, a friend, a relative, self-destructing? Regardless of who it was, to witness someone's self-destruction is a horrific experience.

Perhaps your shake-your-head point in time was the day you found yourself over forty and unemployed. And this layoff had come after many years of devoted service to the owners of the company. Or, this loss of work had come after years of repeatedly going to a job you really didn't care for, but only continued to go to day after day because you needed a job to take care of your family.

Perhaps you shook your head in disbelief when, having finally exhausted all means of juggling your finances to pay that huge note on the house your mate or your children "just had to have" you found yourself faced with foreclosure and eviction.

Evicted from a home you had scrimped and saved and did without to get enough money to barely squeeze by on the down payment required to buy it in the first place.

Friends, who have faced financial difficulties have told me about the experience of going outside to leave for work only to find their car (the one the kids *had really wanted!*) had been repossessed.

These are examples of the harrowing experiences that can leave us feeling as though we are standing in a desert alone.

But that assumption (that we are alone) is far from the Truth.

The Truth is, no matter what, God is there, God is always present.

Let's talk about how we can know God is there — *know that God is there*, when you feel as though you have been kicked in the gut, when you feel as though your legs have been knocked from under you, or when it seems like all has been loss.

We can, in our lifetime, make so many sacrifices, for so many people, so many times, and for so long a time that it can seem like we don't even exist.

And, we live this way, as though our needs and our wants must take a back seat to the needs and wants of others, without a conscious awareness that we even have this mind-set. Living this way, as though this is the way life is supposed to be.

What does one do to change this way of thinking and behaving?

First, a person must realize they are following this pattern of living.

And, how does one develop this awareness?

By self-searching. By taking a deep long look within.

And, by letting this deep long look within be neither critical nor judgmental of the behaviors previously displayed or currently being displayed.

Self-Searching

Activity:

In order for Truth to be revealed we must first know that a problem exists and the true nature of the problem.

Previously I talked about how sometimes difficult information is shrouded in what is called denial as a way of protecting us from that which it is just too difficult to acknowledge.

Remember that?

Well, could it be, that as you read this, you are shrouded in such a veil of denial?

Take a deep breath. Blow it out. You learned how to breathe as a means of contacting God in chapter 1.

Practice—centering, gathering, yourself. Here. Now.

And, reflect upon the following questions.

What have you been caught-up in? What have you been fixed upon? What, in your life, has kicked you in the gut? Is someone you care about self-destructing before your very eyes? Has your trust been betrayed? Do you feel knocked down, dragged about and beat up?

Take a few moments now to reflect upon what has gone on in the past, as well as that which is currently happening in your life.

And remember, you are God's own precious gift. God wants you at peace. God wants you to experience serenity.

In order to make this a reality, to experience the peace which passes all understanding, many health care experts recommend that we take certain steps.

One of these steps is to allow yourself, with the help of God, to think about the things that have happened in your life.

When we do this, we give ourselves an avenue to travel upon which will crystallize and make clear how the past has impacted our here and now and that which is currently happening in our lives.

I want you to think about *your* shake-your-head moments in life. Think about the sacrifices *you* have made. Think about the disappointments *you* have experienced.

Have you, like I did, devoted yourself to a certain outcome only to have it "drift away as though it never existed"?

Take a moment now. Be still. Breathe. And then, ask God to reveal to you that which you need to put down on paper.

Ask God to make *your Truth* clear to you.

And then take a deep breath, like we learned to do in the introduction and in chapter 1, and write down what comes to mind.

This is how it looked. This is what occurred. Here are my shake-your-head moments in life; the sacrifices I have made; the disappoint-ments I have experienced; and, the people who were taken care of, first, by me. To the best of my ability, I allow myself to remember and give myself permission to write down, a description of who and what has taken priority in my life. (Note: Just make a list now, nothing else. Later we will go deeper into how you felt; what you did; and what occurred as a result of your sacrifices.)

Good job. Congratulate yourself for having the courage to hang in there! Even if you didn't write a thing on the page, you are still reading this book, which means you want peace of mind; you want serenity. Take a deep breath. Blow it out. Hold on, you can make it! You *can* experience God's Gift: Calmed heart. Quieted (stilled) nerves. Rest.

Activity:

You have identified that which has been going on in your life. You have identified your times of shock, when you gave all, for another; when your gut hurt after being let down; and when, just as water, your dreams slipped through the fingers of your cupped hand.

And now I want you to write down what happened as a result of the above occurring. I want you to describe your actions and, to the best of your ability, how you felt.

As an example of what I want you to do, here is a description of what I did when my daughter was expelled from school.

> When I spent all of my money to pay my daughter's tuition and then she started failing, acting out in school, and finally got expelled I couldn't believe what had happened. I walked around in a daze the

first few days. I started calling everyone I knew who I thought could help me change the minds of the people at her school. I started screaming and yelling at people. Late at night, I would cry, all by myself. I tried all sorts of self-reliant solutions (to calm my nerves) — beer, nerve pills, eating too much. I starved myself; raged at my daughter; raged at my son and then apologized. I pleaded with school administrators. I overextended myself at work. I tried to fix my friend's problems. And then I raged some more, apologized some more, felt guilty, and prayed fear-filled prayers. *God do this, do that, make this happen!* Nothing worked. As a matter of fact, most of my solutions made the situation worse.

Does any of this sound familiar to you? Have you behaved in a similar manner? Using the description of my behaviors as an example complete the following.

This is what happened when I had my shake-your-head moment in life. I have:

_____

_____

_____

_____

_____

Here is an example of what happened when I have made those huge sacrifices in life only to have things turn out wrong. I have:

_____

_____

_____

_____

_____

This is what happened when I have had that dream-shattering moment of disappointment in life. I have:

_____

_____

_____

_____

_____

This is what happened when I devoted myself to a certain outcome only to have it "drift away as though it never existed."

_____

_____

_____

_____

_____

You have done a courageous thing hanging in there with me so far. Congratulate yourself. Again, even if you haven't written a thing on the page, the fact that you are still reading this book means that somewhere within your heart of hearts you know that God wants you at peace; you know that God wants you experiencing a sense of serenity. And, you are cooperating by continuing to do the exercises in this book to the best of your ability.

And He will hide me in His abode. He will set me high upon a rock.

—*Psalm 27:5*

Renewal

It is now time to talk about healing. You have listed what you have been caught-up in, what you have been fixed upon, what has kicked you in the gut, the pain of watching someone you care about self-destructing before your eyes, your trust being betrayed, those times of feeling knocked down, dragged about and beat up, the sacrifices, the hurts, and the disappointments. Now it is time to talk about...*How to access God;* it is time to talk about, renewal.

Renewal is that time when you—heartbroken, sitting in a car in the dead of winter, windows frozen over, child expelled from school—let God wrap you, in the warmth of love. And you turn the key in the ignition, never knowing when or how you did it.

> Renewal
> It is that time when you—
> pink slip in hand,
> walk across a busy, four-lane highway—
> your field of vision, from the tears,
> a blinding diamond patchwork quilt of liquid:
> > > reds,
> > > gold,
> > > blues,
> > > silver;
> a stark prism of glass—
> > reach the other side.
> > > Safely.
> > > Intact.
> > > Jostled.
> But, standing on solid ground.
> Firmly fixed, as described in Psalm 1:3,
> *like a tree planted by the rivers of water.*
> You stand there safely, because
> —you let God guide you.

It is that time when you — after the sheriff, eviction notice out-stretched in hand, has moved your belongings from what was your home to the curb — sit there, on the front stairs. Numb. Not knowing what to do. And then, a van arrives — driven by a trusted friend, who moves your things into her garage and says, "You can stay with us until you get on your feet."

And, you, within the deepest reaches of your soul, are reminded: "For he will hide me in his abode in the day of trouble. He will conceal me in the shelter of His tent" (Psalm 27:5).

Activity:

On the previous pages you wrote down descriptions of what you did when you have had your shake-your-head moments in life.

To heal, which is God's Plan for us, we must let go of the hurt.

I've given this some thought. And from what I have been able to observe, many of us don't know how to let go. In addition to this, sometimes within our heart-of-hearts we don't really want to…let go.

It could very well be, that the condition of feeling hurt, like the feel of an old much-worn shoe, has gotten comfortable. And, we resist letting it go; we resist throwing it away.

If any of this rings true for you, I have found what is considered a simple, but not easy, solution. It entails one simple step — that I be *willing to be willing* to let go.

Go back to the previous pages and look at what you wrote down.

And then, I recommend that you fall on your knees, lay on the floor, hold your arms up to the sky, sit in a chair, it doesn't matter where or how you do the following — I implore you to — Just do it.

Say: *I release the pain of, the memory of,* (Put your hurts here). Then say: *I let go and I let God. I let go and I let you, dear God, take care of all that has hurt me.*

But before you begin this activity of prayer, take a deep breath. Blow it out. Do it again. Do this (the breathing exercises you learned how to do in the introduction and in chapter 1) until you begin to feel relatively centered and stable.

Good. Now, you're ready to go on.

Activity :

Surrender—it is about release; it is about, put it into God's hands; it is about, "I can't. God can. I think I'll let God; and, it's about—Let go!

What does this mean? It means, as the Big Book of Alcoholics Anonymous states, you stop fighting *anything or anybody.* And when we do this, we are, in essence, admitting to being powerless.

Now, don't confuse this being powerless with being weak.

On the contrary, it is just the opposite.

When we own (embrace) a state of powerlessness, admit to being powerless over all of the people places and things in our lives, with this admission we are saying that: God has the power. And, once done—this surrendering to God, (which in all of its fullness is being infinitely connected to and with God)—we can then use the real authority invested in us by God. And that authority, is the power to change our thoughts—(our attitude)—about that which is going on in our lives.

When we change our attitude we can then begin to think about and to do that which God would have us do for our self. That's right, our self.

Write down your surrender list. For example. When I surrendered to the Will of God in my daughter's life I wrote a list like this:

- I let go the need to try and fix everything she gets into
- I let go trying to arrange everything
- I submit to what is
- I can't change what *is*—(my daughter's attitude, etc.)
- God can change my daughter
- I let go and let God!

Activity :

Think about this, many times we forget. We forget the sacredness of self.

Each of us, was created by God. Created, I believe, for a distinct purpose: to spread love.

The human journey very often can, if we allow it to, distort this Truth.

As young children the adults in our life will, through errors of judgment, hurt us. They will think and believe in distortions of truth regarding their own worth; a lack, somehow, in their own value. This hurt, this injury, can lead to a belief on our part that we have no value; that somehow we are tainted; that we deserve to be hurt.

And, if we are taught, early on, to take care of, say an alcoholic mother or father, someone assigned by God to cherish us as infants and toddlers, then we sometimes grow to believe that, our only purpose in life is to take care of another, or else cease to exist.

Lie.

This was and is a lie!

Japanese psychoanalyst and author of *The Anatomy of Dependence*, Takeo Doi, says that as babies we are born with the expectation to be cherished, as in "sweetly and indulgently loved."

Look at the word indulgently. It means to:

gently (as in quietly, softly, tenderly) indulge;

pamper, make a fuss over, cocoon from harm's way.

This, is how God designed that we be treated. As, Gift. Valuable. Wanted. Treasure. *This*, is who you are.

Say the following:

I am a creation of God. Sacred. Cherished by God.

Keeping in mind these words as well as the thoughts shared with you in the above paragraph, on the lines below write a note to yourself. Write a note of love. In this note "act as if," as they say in the 12 Step Programs. Act as if you believe you are a gift—valuable, treasured. Let God speak to you through you.

Dear _____ (Put your name on this line.)

_____

_____

_____

_____

_____

_____

_____

_____

Activity:

Stand in front of a mirror that has a good light, one that will give you a good, clear, chest-high view of yourself. Take a deep breath. Blow it out. Do this (the breathing exercise you learned how to do in the introduction) until you feel reasonably centered and present. Now take a deep long look into your eyes in the mirror. Stay with it. Let God look through your eyes at you, giving you the image you are to see. As you look, let your self see the goodness within you. Let your self look upon you as created by God your Creator: whole, intuitive, loving, joyous, intact, healthy, valued, precious, wanted. — You were, after all, chosen to be created by God. Just stay there, for a moment, with this image. You may begin to experience emotions that might be uncomfortable. This is okay. Let them surface. If, perhaps, tears start to well-up, let the tears come. Let them surface and flow. They are healing. You may start to feel sad. That is also okay. You may start to feel scared. That too is okay. Just remind yourself that you are safe.

Say it out loud. I am safe. It is the year _____ (put the year in here) and God is right here with me. I am whole, intuitive, loving, joyous, intact, healthy, valued, precious, wanted. I was created by God.

I recommend that you take 5 minutes per day to affirm yourself in this way.

Activity:

Make an appointment with a trusted and valued friend who has repeatedly shown a respect for your value and worth. Someone who has frequently shown that they have a high regard for you. Take the letter about you that God dictated to you. At this meeting you will read this letter out loud. You will say to your friend: "I wanted to meet with you to tell you that I am," (Then proceed to read aloud the wonderful, affirming truths God touched your heart with that you put into the letter.)

Again, act as if. Act as if you believe yourself to be worthy. Act as if you believe yourself to be as a gift. Act as if you believe yourself as precious in God's eyes. Act as if you believe you were formed by God unique, special, as is, just because you are you. And, as a matter of fact, if you had trouble listening to God when you were writing your letter look at the words you just read: *worthy, gift, precious, formed by God – unique, special, as is* and put those words in your letter.

Start it with – I <u>(Put your name here   )</u> am worthy, a gift from God, precious, formed by God unique, special, as is.

If you, as yet, do not believe this to be true, again act as if, until you do believe this Truth.

The way in which you can begin this process of believing in your worthiness is to say to yourself throughout the day:

> *"I want to believe I am worthy. I want to believe I am a gift from God. I want to believe I am precious. I want to believe I am formed by God unique, special, as is."*

Say this many times throughout the day.

Make appointments with yourself daily to validate yourself in this manner.

After a time you will begin to value yourself at least a 10th of what God values you. And if you can value yourself in just a 10th of how God sees you and cherishes you then you will have what you need to move forward in grace and joy.

Prayer

God here I am. Bruised and torn. It hurts. It still hurts. And, Your Promise is that if I rely on you and you alone all will be well. For this reason, in faith, I come to you with all that has been and is hurting me. I place every shake-your-head moment, every sacrifice, every disappointment, and every pain I have experienced into your hands. I release into your care all my earthly worry and concerns. I let your powerful arms encircle me.

Affirmations

- The power of God is healing me.

- I lack the power to fix —
  (put the name of the person or situation that you are concerned about here)

- God can fix —
  (put the name of the person or situation that you are concerned about here)

- Right at this moment, I turn over —
  (put the name of the person or situation that you are concerned about here)
  to the care of God

- I can't. God can. I let God.

- God wants me healed.

- God is here, right now, with me.

- I let go of the fear.

- I embrace God.

- I turn over to God all my worldly cares.

- I am willing to let the hole in my heart be filled with God's glorious love.

- Love and joy, peace and grace now fill every fiber of my existence.

- I feel the Presence of God.

- I want to be at peace. I want to be at peace. I want to be at peace.

Suggestions For Healing

Access God: Healing

God is just a Breath away. God is always...here. We just forget to call on Him/Her.

Your child got kicked out of school? Bemoan the fact. If tears well-up in the back of your eyes, cry. If a scream finds its way into the base of your throat, holler. Then, suck in your gut. Wash your face. And, do what is in front of you to do. *What* those in the 12 Step programs say is "the next best thing...to do."

Each one of these actions, from bemoaning the fact that your child got kicked out of school to doing what seems to be the "next best right thing to do," is a call to God. And, each time we call on God, whether in a scream or tears flowing we are...praying.

Prayer is being in touch with God. Being in touch with God, means being present: present, in each and every activity I find myself involved in.

Take a deep breath. Blow it out. There. You just accessed God. Do it again. And, as you breathe in say: Breathing in, I calm my body. Breathing out, I let go fear.

Sit quietly, as quietly as you can. Sense the power of God flowing into the top of your head. God's wisdom is filling your mind. God's love is filling your heart.

You now have the mind and heart of God.

Whether you are getting ready to make funeral arrangements for a loved one or attend a hard-earned graduation ceremony, you have all you need for that which is in front of you to do.

Keep breathing. God is just a breath away.

Surrender:

Many times when we hear the word surrender we think about waving the white flag of giving up. Surrender, as in letting go and letting God, is far from that concept.

In actuality the surrender we have referred to in this chapter has been about release. Release and letting go of the reigns of power that we *think* we have.

Think about the prayer, "I surrender to you, Dear God, all my earthly cares and woes."

Does this imply a giving up, or a calling on God for the power we need to get through a situation?

The latter.

It is then that we let go, set free, surrender, stop fighting *"anything or anybody."* And, when we do this, we clear a space within ourselves to receive real power, the power of God.

When we surrender, we submit to; yield to; pray; relinquish the reigns; let go; renounce holding on; and abandon fear. We become humble, a virtue of necessity, which allows us to get on bended knee and experience true humility, which is: the ability to ask for...what I need.

Value Self/Claim Self/ Profess The Worthiness Of Self

Begin with the day, month and year of your birth and begin to count backwards from that date. You are doing this to determine when the previous nine months began. For example: I was born on August 1st. Nine months prior to August 1st was December 1st of the previous year. Each December 1st I celebrate what I call Conception Day. Conception Day, in my mind, is the Date that God — *Conceived of me*, created me, formed me in my mother's womb. Taking the best of my biological father and mother and breathed life into a lifeless form and named her Shirley — teacher, writer, orator — *you shall go forth and proclaim God's goodness. This is your Purpose.*

For many years I let the distortions of Truth that I had been raised with taint the Truth of my birthright. I was totally unaware of the intrinsic beauty of me. I believed what had happened to me, rather than in what God had Created.

I did not value self.

I ate too much, drank too much, worked too much, and expected too much of myself, my children, friends, relatives, and life in general.

That changed when I began to value the sacredness of Creation. I began to understand that: only God Creates; each creation of God is sacred; I have a part in the nurturance of God's creation; and, God wants "these arms and legs (mine) to take care of me, first." With this knowledge I began, to the best of my ability, to: eat right; drink healthy and nourishing substances; work in such a way as to help me rather than hurt me; and, most of all began to allow myself as well as others to be a human being rather than a human doing. I let go of the expectation that we be perfect.

You, are a wonderful, precious, Creation of God. Valuable. Treasured. Created for a distinct Purpose. I invite you to nurture the woman you are. I invite you to nurture the man you are. Remember: nine months prior to the date of your birth God *Conceived of you*, Formed and fashioned you, Breathed Life into you. And, said: Well Done!

Treat yourself as such. God bless.

THREE

Another...Chapter

Another...Promise

❧

HAVE you ever found yourself involved in a situation that just kept you shaking your head? A situation, that for the life of you, you just couldn't make sense out of?

For example: The athlete, in perfect physical condition, who has a debilitating heart attack that cripples him or her. The teenager who was dedicated to God in the womb, but is turning his or her back on all that is sane, good and of God. The woman who betrays a friend she has known since childhood and has literally been with "through thick and thin." The child from the affluent family who robs a convenience store. The respected minister of one of the biggest churches in town who is found guilty of absconding with funds from the church.

Each of these people has relatives and friends who, for the life of themselves, can't make sense out of what has occurred.

These relatives and friends probably have called on God. They more than likely have prayed but at times their spirits might have been so low they could only come up with: "Lord are You listening; can You hear me? Where are You Lord?"

Sound familiar?

It does to me.

One of *my* greatest Faith journeys with God making sense out of no sense came when both my children were addicted to alcohol as well as other drugs.

Year after year I prayed to God with varying degrees of faith. I'd pray for help, turn the problem over to God, then snatch it back.

God never did what I wanted done fast enough for me. Oh, I prayed, but in the back of my mind (sometimes not so back of my mind) I would be wailing: "Where are you God? Why haven't you fixed this? When are you going to heal my children?"

It wasn't until years later, when I had been appointed as director of a drug and alcohol treatment program, that I understood, truly understood, the *why* of the years of pain and turmoil.

Wisdom takes time to be developed.

Wait.

God in all his wisdom wanted me to know first-hand about the disease of alcoholism and drug addiction.

Wait.

From my own foray into beer, food, and nerve pills I understood on a personal level how it felt to be addicted to some type of substance. But I needed to know how the *parents* of a person addicted to alcohol and or drugs felt. And so, I...waited.

God wanted an expert to minister to his children.

Wait.

And for this reason, God allowed *me* to walk in their shoes.

What are you waiting on?

In this chapter we will talk about times of confusion, how to find God, and how to find the answer. We will talk about the concept and the process of, wait. We will talk about *how* to wait. Many times we are so confused by the things that have happened or are happening in our lives that we can seem to be in a barren wasteland (the desert) alone. It is during those times that we need to be reassured God is with us. We need what those of us of the Christian faith call Blessed Assurance. And what the Jewish faithful call Devekut—bound to the Divine through everything we do—a God-consciousness, communion with God, being at peace because God is in charge: *my essence is still and firm in God.*

No matter what one calls it, to find this Blessed Assurance, which, in my opinion, is a synonym for faith—faith in God, there are sound realistic actions that one can take.

This chapter will outline those actions. And I, as well as the trusted servants of God that I sought out for counsel, have found that taking these actions allows us to go from being confused to confident…baffled to believing…puzzled to perceiving God's presence…and, from perplexed to powerful.

"No…!"

She looked out of that window yet one more time. Nothing. At ten o'clock she had been mad. At midnight she had been furious. At one she began to be a little uneasy. At two she was somewhat alarmed. At three her mind was racing: *He's alright. I know he's alright, but boy am I going to let him have it when he does show up!* At four she was terrified. At five: "I'm sorry M'am, but there is a 24 hour waiting period before we can file a missing person report." At six she was terror-stricken: *Should I call his mother? What if he got in a car wreck? Maybe someone tried to rob him? Oh, Lord, the baby, and Jeffie are going to be awake soon.* At seven she looked out of that apartment window again, *there it was*, Oh, how great and good that little white car looked! She ran out of the apartment rushing the elevator down the ten flights to the ground floor. When she finally made it to the first floor she squeezed herself out of the door before it had actually opened wide enough for her to exit. As she approached the car she was scared, she couldn't see anyone sitting behind the steering wheel. When she got closer she was able to determine that a body was slumped across the front seat. *It was him.* Oh my God, is he alright?! Having forgotten her car keys upstairs, she began knocking furiously on the side window. Thank God, he stirred. Some more knocking and he sat upright. He opened the door on the passenger's side. It was then that she saw it. A woman's white purse. He had been using it as a pillow.

Some time later, thinking back on it, she could recall a fleeting moment of underlying incredulence, perhaps it was hysterics. *Everything matched:*

the car, the purse, his shirt, they were all white. A blizzard of white. If it had been in the winter, instead of July, the snow would have completed Dante's inferno of white. Although it seemed like an eternity, in one split second she sat in the car, opened the purse, and heard herself asking; "Who does this belong to?" It was then she caught sight of the keyring buried within the hodgepodge of articles most women carry in their purse. Daystar Hotel, Room 101.

Beth had no idea how or when she got her next-door neighbor to baby-sit the children. What she does remember is telling her husband: *Take me there. Take me to the Daystar Hotel. Now!*

When she got there she walked zombie-like to room 101, put the key in the door, turned the key, turned the knob on the door, and there she was, the woman her husband of two short years, and the father of their two beautiful children had slept with and most likely had sex with the night before. The woman never woke up. She lay there. Sound asleep. Breathing evenly like the infant Beth had just left with her neighbor. She told her husband; *Let's go.* And with that, Beth closed the door on the hotel room and life, as she had known it to be.

She remembered her husband stopping at the front desk giving the clerk instructions and a message for the woman they had just left in the room.

They drove home in silence.

There was a Catholic Church directly across from their apartment building. Beth found herself sitting in that church on that morning. The Mass was recited in Latin. She didn't understand a word but what she did understand within each layer of her mind, her body, and her soul was that God was there. She knew intrinsically that God was taking care of her. She knew that, within this situation that made no sense…

God would prevail.

No! She inwardly screamed. *We could still be considered newlyweds! Ned is so-o-o good with the children! He scrubs my floors every week. We were married in the church. I pray every day. I don't make a decision without first asking God what I should do. I have done everything my pastor, the books, and Ned's mother said a good wife should do.*

God will prevail.

What does a person do when, to the best of their ability, they have followed the teachings, the guidelines, of all that is considered and said to be precious and good and, yet, their life journey goes into a tailspin?

What do people do when they continue to walk the walk of God, Christ, Allah, Buddha, their Higher Power, and no matter how hard they try, the problem they have been praying about persists?

Scripture tells us: "They that Wait On the Lord Shall Have Their Prayers Answered."

In each and every struggle there is a lesson. We learn something.

The solution, the answer to the question "Why God?" may not be readily forthcoming. Many times we have to wait to discover the gift of the trial, but while we wait, God is always present. *"I will not leave you, nor forsake you"* (Heb 13: 5 KJV).

This is God's promise to us.

When Jesus was in the Garden of Gethsemane he asked Peter, *"Can you not wait one hour with me?"*

So, too, like Peter, God is asking you: *"Can you not wait one hour with me?"*

The while that you are waiting for the solution, for the answer, to be made known is another part of your journey of faith. It is you, waiting *with* God. And what better place can one ever be than with God, especially in times of trouble?

God's promise is that God's grace will be with us throughout any and all painful and confusing situations.

Our journey of faith requires us to believe that and to be willing to still our self in our belief in God, while and when God asks: *Can you not wait one hour with me?*

Waiting

Activity:

You did it all right, just like you had been taught. Prayed. Believed. Walked the walk. Talked the talk. And yet, it still turned out wrong. Your life, some portion of it, like the young mother in the story and mine on various occasions, is in a tailspin.

I want you to talk to God right now.

Center yourself in prayer to the best of your ability. Think about the following questions. Then tell God all about it.

What situation(s) has/have had you, just as a twister in a tornado, reeling?—*A storm stomping through your mind.* What is it that has been going on in *your* life that you can't make sense out of no matter how hard you try? What have *you* been waiting on? What, are *you* confused about? What, have *you* been waiting for God to fix, to make right? Tell God.

Dear God, try as hard as I can, I don't understand how you could have let

_____

_____

_____

_____

_____

_____

_____

_____

happen.

You have just opened up to God.

It was *for you* rather than for God that you expressed your confusion and perhaps anger and sadness over what has happened or is happening in your life.

God didn't need to be told what was going on. God already knew.

When we risk to *tell* God it is for *our* benefit.

It is this telling God what we just don't understand, or are confused or mad about that clears a space to welcome God.

When we do this, clear a space for God, we receive the grace of God. Pain doesn't necessarily leave. However, solutions appear. And in this state of grace answers are forthcoming.

Activity

Take a moment to center yourself in prayer. Review the breathing exercises in the introduction and chapter 1. Take 3 minutes and do as instructed there. Then come back to this section.

Good. Now let's begin.

Look around you. Look at what you just wrote down. Look at your life as it is; not, as you want it to be but as it currently is today. That thing that you are confused about or "just can't make sense out of," is, on today, a reality in your life. And, I want you to make friends with what is.

To learn to make friends with, to embrace, the hell that was going on in my life at one time, I learned to express and to affirm in my life the following. And, I prayerfully request that you say and do the same.

God, I don't know how you could have let — (read out loud what you wrote above) — *happen, but since you allowed it and I can't change it, it is the best thing for me and everybody concerned. Please bless me to say, in faith; I wouldn't have it any other way, and then to believe this in my heart.*

Sit with this for a moment. You might be saying: Is she crazy?! How can it be the best thing for me and my child who is killing herself with drugs?

If you feel this way, I understand how you feel. I too felt this way when this concept was introduced to me. I asked the person who invited me to say this: ARE YOU OUT OF YOUR MIND?

But as the years progressed, and I got better, I came to believe in this.

I came to believe in a power other than and greater than myself.

I came to believe, truly believe, in God.

And, on today, I can say from the deepest recesses of my heart about my life circumstances as they are revealed to me on a daily basis: Since God has allowed this to happen, and I can't change it, it is and must be the best thing for me and all concerned.

And, then…I pray for more faith.

More faith in God's ability to take care of everything that goes on in God's world. That includes murder, rape, unplanned pregnancies, drug addiction, death, homelessness, failures in school.

It is called Acceptance.

Until I was able to accept life on life's terms, I could not truly manifest the presence of God in my life.

And when I block God's presence in my life I begin to think I have to stand alone, all by myself.

And when I think I have to stand alone, all by myself, I begin to believe that *I have to fix it* — (whatever it is).

And when I begin to believe that I have to fix it all by myself, waiting is nowhere on my agenda and I start to rush around at terrifying speeds.

And when this occurs I can find no Serenity and no peace of mind. Thereby robbing myself of the comfort that comes from a relationship with God based on Trust: Trust, and faith that all is and will be well.

I rob myself of the Truth that…*Now faith is the substance of things hoped for, the evidence of things not seen.* Hebrew 11-1(KJV).

Activity

The problem, that challenge, as I like to refer to it, is on today a reality in your life.

You woke up today and found — it's not any better than it was yesterday. She is/he is still running around and cheating on me; using drugs; failing in school; staying out all night; stealing; fighting.

Since God could surely change what is going on in your life, what reason, what purpose could there possibly be for God to allow the situation to remain as it is?

Think back to another trying moment in your life. What did you learn from it? Take a deep breath. Blow it out. Center yourself in prayer and consider that time.

Last _____ I went through _____
    (year, month, night, etc.)

_____

_____

_____

_____

_____

_____

And, the lesson that I learned from this experience was:

_____

_____

_____

_____

_____

You are doing a good job. In Ecclesiastes 3 we learn that there is a reason, a time, and a purpose for everything. What could be the purpose "under God's heaven," for that which you wrote down in the first activity in this chapter? What possible good could come from this going on in your life?

Look for your lesson. Look for the good that God always brings about from those situations that we just can't make sense out of no matter how hard we try.

I want you to do a let's pretend exercise right here: Let's pretend that you are helping a friend go through what you are going through. What would you tell him or her? You would probably say something similar to this: *Girl,(man), you know God can make all things turn out right. Just look for the good in this situation. Going through this you are gaining wisdom. You will be able to help someone else when* they *go through this. You are becoming an expert on cancer research. You could go before congress and get new laws made. You can become a teacher. You could…*

And, the list could and does go on and on.

Stay open. Stay open to finding your lesson, the Gift, God's Divine Providence — that condition whereby God permits the horrible and/or vile so He/She can (from that very situation) give birth to, create, goodness.

Activity:

Look for God. Take a deep breath. I'll bet you are saying: "She sure wants me to breathe." That's right, I do. Breathing is a form of prayer and it is the first line to life.

As you breathe, say: I know my God is here.

And, as you breathe, allow yourself to create a gratitude list. A gratitude list consists of those things we have and use on a daily basis that if they were missing the quality of our life would somehow be affected.

The way in which I create *my* gratitude list is to allow myself to become consciously aware of and to say thank you for each and every aspect of my existence for one hour of the day.

Try it. This is how it is done. When I blink my eye, turn my head, pick up my pen, hear a sound in the background, swallow, sit in a chair, rise from the chair, empty my bladder, have a bowel movement, speak, touch something, taste a sip of coffee, frown when something is too bitter, smile when it taste good, bend my elbow, move my foot, point my finger, hold a pencil firmly, turn on the lights, open the refrigerator, take food out to defrost, hug a friend, think about and miss a loved one who is dead, open the door to my car, turn the key in the ignition, cough, sneeze, rub my eye, pick up my child, use the telephone, go get a checkup, Breathe, and, on and on and on—the list is infinite, never-ending—I say…Thank You.

We do these things most often without thinking about it. We, take them for granted.

When I am going through a trial I schedule "gratitude breaks." I actually put it on my calendar that at, say, 2 o'clock today, I will allow myself to recognize and say thank you to God for each and every thing that I do and experience between the hours of 2pm and 3pm.

The fact that I am able to keep breathing, my actual lifeline to life, without even thinking about that action proves to me many things. A primary and very fundamental truth it proves is that God is in charge and loves me 100% of the time.

When things "get tough" I often forget about the unceasing all-powerful love of God. It is then that I need reminding that *God is always present*. And, my gratitude breaks are the times when I become aware of all of the things that just could not be, other than by and of and through God.

Take gratitude-breaks. All you have to do is blink your eyes, take a deep breath and look all around you.

And, when you say thank you, affirm out loud: God is right here with me.

Activity:

So, too, like Peter, God is asking us: "*Can you not wait one hour with me?*"

It is a certainty that as we move about completing our day-to-day pursuits we are waiting. How that wait looks is totally and completely our choice.

Sometimes our wait looks like this: Head hurting and nerves frayed, we travel through our day chanting complaints of "ain't it awful," waylaying friends as well as family with our misery as we drag along this doom and gloom wherever we go.

However, there is another way a hallowed, devout, and pure way that we can wait for the blessing of healing. Let's talk about that. Let's talk about the purity of the waiting process.

"Can you not wait one hour with me?"

What, could actually be going on as we wait for a certain outcome? Could it be that God is just a big old mean God who wants us to suffer?

I think not.

As I have traveled the course of my journey I have found just the opposite. Charitable, benevolent, are just two of the terms that come to mind as I think back about the way in which God has walked (sometimes carried) me through the travels of my life.

If you can, envision a loving kind Teacher (Instructor) of life. *This* has been, and is, the God of my Journey.

This God has taught me that I only have to, live through, one day at a time. As a matter of fact, only one second at a time.

This same loving God has taught me that no matter how horrible the situation I find myself in it is only one of the things — one of the activities, one of the situations, one of the pursuits, one of the endeavors — call it what you will — in which I am involved. My day, from first waking moment until the closing of eyelids at night, is a cornucopia of activity. What I have found myself doing, and what I am learning — through God's Instruction — to change, is a tendency to fixate on, paralyze, make rigid, my grip upon that problem that is running me crazy.

What my God has taught me to do to counteract this tendency and to bring a modicum of sanity to my day is to do what is in front of me to do.

Here is an example of what I mean: The sink is full of dirty dishes. Visualize a woman standing in front of the sink staring out the window that is above it thinking about the chaos in her life — her daughter is on drugs, her husband is cheating on her, her son is in jail — *you* name it. No matter what the situation, it represents chaos to her.

Like this woman, many years ago, my grip upon a problem, was rigid. My every waking thought was colored by and steeped in the situation.

On today, what I am learning to do and what God is prompting me to share with you, to do, is to live in the moment by doing what is in front of me to do: the dishes. And, leave the rest up to God.

God makes known to me what I am to think about and do by the way in which events unfold throughout my day.

When I do this, I am surely waiting with and on God.

By putting the problem in perspective — (it is just one of the things that is going on in my life not the only thing that is going on in my life) — I deflate, take away, its power to dominate my life circumstances.

Try this: Tomorrow when you awake, as part of your good-morning, saying thank you to God for waking you up ritual, make a commitment to live each second of the day as it is revealed to you. Doing as Jesus instructed the disciples to do, especially Peter, when they were in a boat in troubled waters off the shores of Gennesaret: Keep your eyes fixed on God, neither straying (looking) to the left nor to the right but keeping your eyes fixed upon Jesus. This same passage of the Bible goes on to recount:

> And when Peter had come down out of the boat, he walked on water to go to Jesus. But when he saw that the wind was boisterous he was afraid; and beginning to sink he cried out, saying, "Lord save me!" And immediately Jesus stretched out *His* hand and caught him, and said to him *Oh you of little faith, why did you doubt?* And when they got into the boat, the wind ceased. Then those who were in the boat came and worshiped Him, saying, "Truly You are the Son of God."[1]

So therefore on today: start out with prayer; brush your teeth; wash your face; eat your breakfast; wash the dishes; go to work, if you are employed outside the home; make that telephone call; laugh, cry; hope; believe; think; feel; sit quietly in prayer and make plans (making sure to stay away from planning the outcome. *Outcomes are up to God*); live life on life's terms as it is revealed to you throughout the day. Saying, "Lord save me!"; then leave the rest up to God.

---

[1] The Holy Bible, New King James Version, (Nashville, Tennessee: Thomas Nelson, Inc.) 1982

Activity

Blink your eye. Take a deep breath — (there she goes again, telling us to breathe). Sit quietly for a moment. Think about what you would consider as being one of the worst moments in your life.

What type of demeanor did you display? While you were going through the challenge did you ever take on a quality of lightness about yourself? Were you ever amazed at the fortitude you displayed? Were you in amazement at your tenacity — how you hung in there no matter how much you teeter-tottered and bobbed around when you would get what you considered to be the equivalent of being kicked-in-the-gut?

What you are remembering is called Grace. You are remembering being in a state of grace.

Right now, where you sit or stand or lay, God is with you and blessing you. The reason I asked you to blink your eyes and take a deep breath is that your state of grace, God, is just that close to you. In the blink of an eye, grace, miracle, is yours for the accepting.

Prayer

Dear God:

I come to you bruised and torn.

As a child comes to a parent with a broken toy to mend, I come to you with my broken heart.

It hurts. I can't fix it. Only you and you alone have the power to make it all right.

I ask you for the grace to live with that which is going on in my life.

You have taught me, through life circumstances, to neither deny what is going on nor to wallow in doom and gloom.

So I ask for the ability (the grace) to say "Ouch!" when it hurts; to cry; to feel the pain.

And once done, this Clearing-A-Space-For-You, (which I have created by opening up the door to and acknowledging my grief and thereby embracing the pain), I ask for the grace to wash my face; to say: Lord save me!; to look for the blessing; to look for the rainbow; to Look for the Miracle.

Affirmations

🖎 God is everywhere. God is everywhere I need God to be. I know God is here. God is right here with me. God never leaves me. I am not alone.

🖎 God is with my loved ones too — God is with my: mother, father, sister, brother, husband, wife, son, daughter, friend.

🖎 God's Eternal Love is filling every fiber of my being.

🖎 God's Wisdom is filling my mind.

🖎 I let go confusion and embrace God. (3 Xs)

🖎 I *Look* by Faith rather than by sight.

🖎 Martha prayed 40 years for her son; I, too, can wait on the Lord.

🖎 I feel the warm healing balm of God's Grace flowing through every inch of my being.

🖎 God's Healing Grace is coursing through my veins.

🖎 I feel the tension relax in my muscles; God's love is flowing through every muscle in my body.

🖎 I know that God will make sense out of this struggle.

🖎 Every *thorn* has a Rose, I look for the Rose; I look for the Miracle.

Suggestions For Healing

Practice Makes Power

Remind yourself, often, that you don't have to do it like a ballerina.

Many times, we can stop ourselves from going forward because we want to, demand from ourselves, that we do it perfectly.

Only God is perfect.

We are agents of change. We are instruments of God's will, growing and learning each step of the way, especially during times of hardship and pain.

Be willing to stumble as you attempt to do God's will—that's a form of waiting. God is the teacher. You are the student. The lesson is life.

When you attempt to do something to solve a problem, say to yourself: "I don't have to do it like the ballerina, I just have to do it."

Iyanla Vanzant in her book, *Faith In The Valley*, defines power as the ability to do.

Allow yourself to experience your power, *do something* each and every day. Take a step toward faith.

Strengthened

Throughout this chapter we have talked about waiting with and on God. Power and strength comes in many forms after a time. We get many forms of power and strength that we come to cherish after a time of waiting. We get:

Gold, once purified.

Diamonds, once buffed.

Mix the soil of the earth, some clay, a little sand, and bits of water as needed. Form into bricks, and give time to settle, to solidify. This then becomes the stuff, the foundation, for a sturdy dwelling.

Wait.

The acorn, becomes the Mighty Oak.

Wait.

A small tributary, faithful, waiting, flowing through all types of obstacles remaining faithful to its course becomes part of the mighty Mississippi River which then becomes part of the Gulf of Mexico which then becomes part of the huge powerful Atlantic Ocean.

Wait.

It takes time.

All God's miracles, take time.

And as we wait we are being strengthened.

Each day, throughout the day, take prayer breaks.

When you stop to pray, consciously breathe in the power of God. Say to yourself as you pray: "I am being strengthened. I am being strengthened by the power of God." Let yourself fill-up as you sit quietly in prayer. Fill up from the center of your being, your gut — with faith.

When you have faith, you don't need patience.

Many times when circumstances indicate that we must wait on the healing, wait on the money, wait on the husband or wife to stop hurting the family, wait for the child to stop acting out, we will say: "Lord, I don't have any patience at all."

Guess what? You don't have to have any patience. If you have faith, you have all that you need.

Wait.

Identify The Gift

Sometimes when we are going through a challenging situation, it can seem all-encompassing. It can seem to engulf us.

To get through the situation many times it can be helpful to remember those other challenges, those other times of pain and confusion we have experienced, worked our way through, or as I like to refer to it, *loved our way through*, and are now no longer troubled by.

Think back to that time when you were almost ready to give up, or perhaps did give up. Now ask yourself the big question: Would I give up the lesson? Would I change anything that happened if it meant I had to give up the gift of the lesson learned? Be honest…was the Gift worth it?

Expect A Miracle

As you wait, expect a miracle.

In the Bible it says to "Walk by faith not by sight" (2 Corinthians 5:7 LB).

Train yourself to do this. If your husband or wife comes in drunk, once again, (or, whatever problem you have been praying about rears its ugly head again), feel your pain, say Ouch!. And then immediately recite the prayer of faith. Say: Oh My God, Precious Lord in heaven, this looks bad and I can see no good in this. And so, in trust and with confidence I look by faith rather than by sight. Please, dear God, place the thought that *you* would have me have in my mind right at this very moment. I surrender. I am hurting; I admit that. And… I expect a miracle.

Another...Chapter

Another...Promise

⚮

LIFE twists and life turns. The only constant is change. And it would seem that we are forever in a struggle with this process of change.

At various times we can think we have it "all together," that we have finally gotten things in order, we know where we want to go and we are about the business of getting there. Then, all of a sudden something happens, a life shattering occurrence, that will shake us to our very core.

You know what I'm referring to; we all have had it happen to us:

I'm sorry; your son was found dead this morning."

"When we went in the cancer had spread to your pancreas. I wish I had something better to tell you. But there's nothing else we can do. If the disease follows its course, you have about six months to live."

"No, we can not let her remain here. She has broken every rule at our school; I'm sorry, she can not return!"

"I want a divorce." "But what about the children?" "I'll always be a part of their life, but I just can't live with you anymore."

Since we each, in our own way, have had similar experiences, and most probably will go through situations that will shake us to our very core in the future, the question becomes then, one of, how to *get through* situations like these?

In this chapter we will discuss ways in which we can embrace God's offer to fortify us. We will talk about steps to take that will allow us to experience the presence of God: to truly have a sense of God *being there* for us. We will list and reflect on ways to feel, *actually feel*, God putting the Strength that we need into our spine. We will talk about ways in which we can *let God* be that Shock Absorber, for the soul, that Claudia Jewette refers to in her book as denial. The shock absorber, that I, instead, have come to think of as a glorious transformed state of consciousness, a gift, from God, that buffers us, steels us, so we can remain alive.

And finally, we will learn about ways in which we can Surrender, to what is, and thereby participate in the glorious miracle that God always manifests when God takes a catastrophe and turns it into something that will benefit not only you or me, the person who has gone through the hurtful experience, but one or more of God's other children.

"Turn around and Look at me...!"

White, blinding light. Starched. Stiff. She squinted. From fear, astonishment, hurt, disbelief, anger? No matter what the reason, her eyes hurt; she needed sunglasses. Can the white starched stiffness of a lab coat blind you?

Turn around. Turn around and face me. How dare you turn your back on me! What's this: "I need to get a reading on your thyroid," business? Didn't you just tell me I have cancer? What difference does it make what my thyroid count is! You have just delivered a death sentence to me and now you want to know how well my thyroid is functioning? Turn around and face me!

Thunder beat against the membrane of her eardrums. A piecing internal scream tore a hole in her chest. Some invisible sculptor had sneaked into the room and chiseled her, in the spot where she sat, on the side of the examining table—fixed, for life, in that place.

And now, he wanted to know what her thyroid count was?!

What difference does it make; what possible difference *could it make*?

She sat. And, she sat. It seemed like an eternity. Forever and never all at the same time. Can time stand still and rush ahead? Can one scream and be mute? Can life end and heartbeat and breaths continue? Can light filter through complete darkness? She sat there.

"As I said, we will need to get a complete work-up on your thyroid count. I would like to schedule it as soon as possible. How about tomorrow morning? You will need to fast from midnight."

"What time will you need me there?"

"8:oo o'clock in the morning will be fine."

"Do I need to bring anything?"

"No."

She sat.

"Do you need my nurse to call someone for you?"

"No."

And, she sat.

Surely, that roar of the Atlantic Ocean would explode the thin layer of tissue designed to protect her eardrums. Everything else had, eroded.

That's it. That's what happened. My eardrum was damaged, I didn't hear him correctly, there's something wrong with my hearing!

And, she sat.

"Mrs. Zanders, Mrs. Zanders?"

Hum, she doesn't have white on. I wonder when nurses stopped wearing those crisp starched uniforms, and why?

She felt a gentle touch on that place between her right shoulder and her elbow. And heard, the soft faint touches of a fading, female Irish brogue. "Ms Zanders, I'm going to call your husband."

"No, there's no need for that, I have an errand to run. Oh, look at the time! I'm going to be late. I promised Meg I'd have those sandwiches there by 3: o'clock. Where has the time gone?"

> *"Stand up! Pick up your mat and go home."*
> (Mark 2:11 NAB).

God surely wrapped this woman in the Cloak of love. She heard, on an external level, that according to the test her body had cancer in it. She was allowed to breathe, hear, talk and swallow. What she was not allowed to do, was to take in full measure, the total magnitude of the diagnosis.

God builds into each one of us at birth a filter of information. When the news is too grave, we automatically filter in only that which we can handle at the moment. We continue to filter in information in this way throughout the time of any challenging situation that we find ourselves involved in.

God in His/Her all-encompassing love shielded this woman. God protected her from the sheer magnitude of this information. He, literally became—as He always does at that moment when the news is so agonizing that we must filter, sensor out, its enormity—her "shock absorber for the soul."

Fit Spiritual Condition

Activity:

The way in which we are able to experience the challenges that come into our lives is determined by our spiritual condition.

If we wait until a tragedy occurs to connect with God, we will surely have God there with us. However, if we live in a way that supports a constant state of prayer, then we will be equipped for that challenge in the same way as the person who thinking ahead puts aside water, matches, candles, canned goods, ethyl alcohol, disinfectant, extra blankets, bandages, and splints, "just in case" that forecasted hurricane, or tornado, or flood comes.

Prayer is the number one recommended *unceasing* activity designed to keep us in constant contact with God.

Prayer has been defined as being, in its essence, in contact with God. There are as many forms of being in touch with God as there are people and experiences. How *you* touch bases with God will depend on, to name a few, your upbringing (sometimes), personality, particular inclinations, belief system, past experiences, or personal preferences.

The consensus among theologians and great thinkers alike is that, it doesn't matter so much *how* we pray, what is important is *that* we pray.

Let's talk to God right now.

Prayer is a wonderful preface to all things, to each and every activity throughout the day. And, I recommend that you say the following prayer before you fill out the accompanying suggested prayer schedule.

> Dear God,
>
> Teach me your way. It is my hope and my desire to experience the challenges in my life with unshakable faith. Show me how to do that. With trust I come to you. I want to be willing to sit quietly and listen to you. I want to be willing to pray each day upon awakening. I want to be willing to take prayer breaks, instead of coffee breaks throughout the day. I want to be willing to end my day with a formal prayer of gratitude for each experience I have had on that day. Whether it be an experience I smiled about or cried about, I want to be willing to say thank you. For you, know better than I, what I need. Dear God, please help me. Teach me *Your Way*.

Prayer Diary (Times I plan to pray today)

Complete one of these each day. If you are an early bird, complete it in the morning right after you have said, Good morning God. Thank You for waking me up. Do this **before you begin your daily tasks**.

If you are a night owl complete it at night, a day ahead of time, right before you retire for the evening and just after completing your final prayer where you say to God: Good night. Thank you for being with me throughout the day. Please stay with me during the night.

_____ a:m   _____ p:m

_____ a:m   _____ p:m

_____ a:m   _____ p:m

_____ a:m   _____ p:m

Activity:

Acceptance is another form of prayer, another way to connect with God. The concept of acceptance is a basic way to develop our ability to accept, rather than fight with, the people, places and things that come into our life

Acceptance has very often been confused with being spineless and gutless. And as a result views of acceptance have taken on a faulty sense of clarity.

It, the notion of acceptance, has gotten confused with giving up; burying our heads in the sand, being willing to settle for less than; and, with living a fake or bogus or artificial way of life.

Acceptance is anything but this.

In actuality, acceptance is a reality-based mindset which is strength personified. It is based on meeting head-on the problems in our lives.

And, we cannot accomplish this—living in a state of serenity—unless we first accept each and every circumstance as it is presented to us.

Self-help books galore as well as popular thought in our culture repeatedly stress the importance of being able to flow, bend, and adapt as opposed to struggle.

When we accept, not like, what is actually going on in our life we are placed firmly in the here and now and what is true.

And to be fixed in the here and now, *and what is,* means to be planted (more importantly rooted) in God.

With this setting down comes involvement. Involvement with God, in today. And it is through this involvement that I am able to acknowledge and be a part of *what is* rather than run from or pretend that a certain circumstance doesn't exist.

It is then, that I am with God—and being with God *is the very essence of prayer.*

The question becomes then, how do I get myself to accept, to actually embrace, what is in fact happening in my life no matter how awful it is?

What I have learned is that we strive to develop—by asking for it in prayer—the ability to say: "Lord, I wouldn't have it any other way. I surrender." To be able to say this, but more importantly to believe it, is strength personified.

The ability to do this comes from faith.

And, faith is to know.

We can acquire faith by putting on our *faith-finding* binoculars.

With these binoculars we look back over our life, find, focus on, and magnify those past faith-building experiences.

> Note: This, looking back, to find the faith-building experiences is one of the few circumstances under which I would recommend that you look back. I have found that to look back, under most other circumstances, is to engage in a futile self-defeating exercise. Because, when we live in the past and wallow in old hurts, we abort the present.

That being said, put on your binoculars.

Think back.

Allow yourself to remember, the unexpected news.

Go gently now, (take a deep breath, slowly release it), stay present, stay right here, in this moment, *that's* where God resides.

The thought of going back and opening up old wounds might seem scary. But you can do this! I know you can!

It takes courage, and you have courage. Because, God, the Source of your courage, is right here with you.

And the proof of this courage, and God's eternal presence in your life, is that you made it through every other painful situation you have ever been through.

Right?

Right.

Lessons learned along the way can be painful. But the lessons are where we find our hidden miracles.

Our all-knowing God, in his/her gentle mercy, always creates good from each and every circumstance we go through.

Take a moment to reflect. Write down what you remember. Put down those things, those past day problems and challenges, those unexpected events that have occurred in your life.

_____

_____

_____

_____

_____

_____

_____

Congratulations, you did it. Take a deep breath; take several of them. Feel the presence of God.

Now allow yourself to remember how God saved you. What happened to bring you through the turmoil? List the miracle(s) you now know happened during (and as a result of) the misery and perhaps hardship. Remember, you have on your *faith-finding* binoculars.

_____

_____

_____

_____

_____

_____

_____

You did a great job. God is right here with you. Let's continue. Remember to breathe.

Activity:

Ask God For Direction

It says in Matthew 7:8, "Ask and you shall receive."

That seems such a simple statement. Uncluttered. Non-confused. Simple to do.

In five easy to understand words, *ask and you shall receive*, that scripture tells us what to do and what the results will be.

Since the way to find peace and serenity, as well as *the answer* to any challenge-any question, has been made so clear and succinct by God, why does our life often seem like one big mask of confusion when a tough time occurs?

Could it be that we begin to run so fast, away from what is happening, that it is impossible for a solution to catch up with us? Is it a lack of faith? Do we so mistrust our Creator that we stop believing God will save us? Do we get in our own way, blocking God's grace? What is it that stops us from knowing what to do? What is it that prevents us from immediately seeking God's solution (*Asking so we can receive*)? — Anger? Frustration? Fear?

I know for me, when I am angry with a friend it is very hard for me to ask that friend for help. It is as though I am locked away from that person by a barrier of petulance. I am mad at them, and I don't want to hear anything they have to say! I shut my mind and my heart to them — Because, they did — in my mind — something hurtful to me.

Could we, unconsciously, be doing the same thing to God?

A tough time occurs, (a situation that rocks us), we believe that God is all-powerful, this being the case, we believe that God somehow caused this or at best didn't stop it from happening.

My God my God why *hath Thou forsaken me?!*

And ergo, consequently, goes the source of my anger.

I know God is my best friend. With all of my other friends at some point and time I have been mad at them. And although I fear admitting it, it stands to reason that perhaps, just perhaps, when tough times occur I get mad at God, too.

All, some, or none of the above underlying ways of thinking or believing could be the reason why we find ourselves scared and confused—not knowing which way to turn or what to do when trouble occurs.

The reason really doesn't matter. What does matter is to connect with God. Because with God, is the only place where we will find a solution, the real solution.

Whether we are running from the truth or are mad at God the way to peace and an ultimate solution is to stop.

That's right, stop!

Stop running, if only just for a moment.

Sit with the pain, again if only just for a moment.

If you are mad at God. Stop. Stop and let yourself admit it.

Then stop for another moment and ask: Has God always protected me and provided me with my highest and greatest good?

If your journey has been anything like mine, your answer will be a resounding yes.

Once you have gotten the answer to that question do as you would do with any good friend. Let the love you have shared outweigh any current turmoil. And begin to trust, trust the history of the love you share.

Trust God.

Say what is on your mind and move on.

For example, say: *I sure hate that this has happened and I don't understand why or how you let this happen. But Lord, my faith resides in you, and I come to you seeking forgiveness—for anything I might have thought, said, or done that lacked love. I also come to you seeking solutions. I ask for your help.*

Now, having unblocked the channels of communication…. Ask God for the answers. *Ask and you shall receive.* Seek out information—to secure a solution. Here is a suggested prayer.

Dear God: I seek your help. I ask you *what*, is the best thing for me to do, in this situation, to take care of me? I surrender to what is. I no longer want to fight with this situation. I know you are leading me to people places and experiences that will glorify you, and good, as well as help me. As I pray, I ask you to place in my mind the course of action you would have me follow. Into my mind, out of my fingertips, and onto the page let flow your solution. As I learned in Matthew 7:8, *seek and you shall find.* I seek your help. Now, Lord. Now.

Here is a detailed description of a current day problem that is causing me pain.

(Note: Put only one problem down. If you have more than one troubling situation going on in your life at this time, make a copy of the pages of this activity and fill in one problem on each set of papers. In that way you will have one problem listed, but more importantly <u>one set of solutions</u> for each problem. Using this method, allows you to see clearly the path upon which God wants you to travel for each situation you are faced with. Remember, all of the issues might seem very important and might be straining your nerves to the ninth inch, but humans are designed to work on one thing at a time. Choose one to work on first, then another, and so forth, until you have a plan of action for each troubling situation.) Be gentle with yourself.

_____

_____

_____

_____

Question : What to do first?

In the 12 Step Programs there is a slogan that reminds us to do "First things first." No matter how confusing the situation, there is a first line of action, there is one thing to do first that will make the doing of the other things more efficient. Take a deep breath. Blow it out. Let God guide you. Think. Write down what comes to mind.

_____

_____

_____

_____

Question: Where are the people/agencies/organizations that might provide me with the help I need?

For example: If, you too, as the woman in the story have been given a diagnosis of a serious illness, where do you need to go to get the information you will need in order to save your spiritual, mental, emotional and physical life? Take a deep breath. Breathe in wholly. And...

Let God guide you. Jot down what comes to mind.

_____

_____

_____

_____

Question : What do I need to let go of?

Are there any old mindsets that you need to let go of? For example: Are you still hanging on to beliefs that you had as a young child, teenager, young adult, single person, married person, working person, etc.? Are you trying to fit today's problems/challenges into yesterday's solutions? Are you trying to force what was into what is?

To illustrate the point: 75 year old legs, no matter how fit they are, walk run bend and flex differently than when they were 35 year old legs. Are you still trying to *make them* do as they used to? And, for that matter, who or what are you *still trying to make* do what it, he, or she, used to do?

Stretch your arms out in front of you with the palms of your hands facing upward and your fingers spread open wide. Sit or stand or lie there for a moment in this position. This is the Release/Receive position. It is a position of offering—*I offer and release that which hurts. And within the same instant, the same breath, I am open to* receiving *that which heals.*

Prayer. This *is*, a profound place of prayer. —*A prayer of faith.* And from this mighty place of prayer will come thoughts. Thoughts about, what you need to let go.

Write down what comes to mind.

_____

_____

_____

_____

_____

Question : What do I need to grab hold of?

God has provided you with *today's solutions*. While maintaining the above position of prayer, allow yourself to think about the following:

What, in *this* journey, do you need to grab hold of in order to survive? As a means of helping you answer that question look at what God has just touched your heart to "let go." (See what you wrote above.) Clinicians say that whatever we let go of leaves a hole, a vacant, unsound spot, and it must be filled. Left open, more than likely, it will just fill up with the same old familiar, now no longer serviceable, mind-set, trait, or method of handling situations.

Think opposite, opposite of whatever you are now doing, that the above question helped you to realize you needed to "let go of."

If, for example, you "used to" rely on mama, daddy, a husband, etc. to *do* things for you, could it be, that God is, nudging you, to grab hold of the trait of taking care of yourself?

Here's another illustration. If, your first inclination, in a new and uncertain situation has been one of being fearful, could it be that God is nudging you toward, encouraging you to, grab hold of a mind-set that allows you to grab hold of faith, as a first response to the new and unfamiliar?

Fill in *your* blanks. What do *you* need to grab hold of? Maintain the prayerful position of Release/Receive. Take a deep breath. Center yourself in God, and then fill in the blanks.

You can do this! I know you can.

_____

_____

_____

_____

_____

Activity:

Create a support system for yourself

Many times when we are experiencing the challenges of life we need a prop, an abutment, a brace. We also need assistance, help, relief, succor. From time to time we may need someone who will defend us, endorse us, advocate for us, and—back us up. We can be experiencing so many emotions regarding "what we are going through," that we are not able to, on a consistent basis, tap into what is most probably a fine intellect, and a very good problem-solving ability. In a review of the literature on thinking versus feeling, I found that some theorists suggest that it is impossible to think and feel at the same time. Many times we are feeling so strongly about what is going on it becomes difficult to think and make good decisions. And that, is one of the primary purposes of having a good support system in place. When you go to get information that you perhaps might feel sad, mad or scared about, you need a back-up. Don't worry about the need to have a support system making you appear weak and/or ineffective. Once you have gone through what you are now facing, you can in turn be *that* support, later on, for someone else. You know the idiom, "Unless you have walked in my shoes, you can't know what I've gone through?" Well, you *will* have walked in their shoes and you will be able to be of real support to them. Just as the person is who you now allow to be there for you.

"Ask and you shall receive."

Question: Who do I need to help me with this current situation?

Brainstorm. Put down the type of support that it appears you *might* need. For example: Will you need someone who is well versed in the medical, legal, and/or mental health field? Will you need a professional cohort, someone who is well abreast of the comings and goings, of your particular profession? Will you need the support of someone who has already had cancer or some other type of serious physical illness, a child killed, a child/mate incarcerated, or a parent die; or, a person who has lost a job, been fired, downsized, been evicted, experienced foreclosure proceedings, etc? Generically name those people, support groups, and/or agencies, those "experts," that will be able to listen and hear for you, while you are going through your feelings.

There is a spiritual concept and term most often associated with those who follow the Christian Tradition. The concept and term is Paraclete. I've used it before in this book. A Paraclete is believed to be the Holy Spirit interceding for you in the form of a person: An intercessor, a "Comforter," an advocate, someone who will mediate for you, someone who will step in for you when you need a helping hand. You are choosing a "thinking" Paraclete for yourself. He or she is just waiting for you. *Ask and you shall receive.* Take a deep breath. Blow it out. Write down <u>who</u> you might need.

_____

_____

_____

_____

_____

Question: Where am I likely to find these people?

Again, brainstorm. Ask yourself: are any of these people in my family, my circle of friends, my church, my place of employment, at a hospital, in the jail/penal system, within the court system? Is there a support group already in existence for persons who are experiencing what I am going through? Is there a 12 Step Program? Does the yellow pages contain a list of agencies that might help me? Are there any agencies such the Volunteer Information Assistance Center that would have a storehouse o f information regarding various social services agencies? Go on a fact-finding search. Remember: *"Seek, and you shall find."*

This activity requires you to think. In order to be able to think rather than just feel feelings that will interfere with the doing of this activity, God wants you to...
Pray. Breathe. Believe. Think.

_____

_____

_____

_____

_____

Activity:

Do the footwork

Some of us are real good at getting on our knees and praying. What we stumble through and seem scared of, actually intimidated by, is the implementing of that which we are led to do in prayer. It would be good to remember what is on page 60, in the big book of Alcoholics Anonymous: "Many of us exclaimed, 'What an order! I can't go through with it.' Do not be discouraged. No one among us has been able to maintain anything like perfect adherence to these principles. We are not saints. The point is, we are *willing* to grow along spiritual lines. The principles we have set down are guides to progress. We claim spiritual progress rather than spiritual perfection."

That appears to be a good message to remember at this juncture of our journey of developing a "fit spiritual condition." Seek progress rather than perfection.

At first, take tiny baby steps in your attempt to actually do that which God would have you do in this situation. Create a time schedule (a doable time schedule), one that you can realistically follow. For example: You could write down that you will *do something* for from 15 minutes to 60 minutes daily to actually get the footwork done. (Note: it is very important to write down your plans of action, rather than committing them to memory, because we "forget," if they are only committed to memory.)

Footwork Log # 1

Remember. Prioritize your actions. There is always a first step that needs to be taken, that will often, and most likely, lead you to the next step, and the next, and the next, until the journey has been completed.

You can do it!

Pray. Take a deep breath. Center your self in God. And, fill out your list.

Action to be taken	Date:	Time:
_____	_____	_____
_____	_____	_____
_____	_____	_____
_____	_____	_____
_____	_____	_____
_____	_____	_____

Footwork Log #2

Results of Footwork Done (Log # 1) & Needed Follow-up

<u>Results</u>	<u>Follow-up action to be taken</u>	<u>Date/Time</u>
————	————————————————	————
————	————————————————	————
————	————————————————	————
————	————————————————	————
————	————————————————	————
————	————————————————	————
————	————————————————	————
————	————————————————	————
————	————————————————	————
————	————————————————	————

Activity:

Believe

This is the final recommended activity designed to keep you in fit spiritual condition. And, it is thought to be a most critical one.

It is a very simple activity but not an easy one. I recommend that you do just one thing: Believe. Believe in God and believe in—you. That's it. As said before: Simple but not easy.

You can develop this ability to believe by remembering to recognize and acknowledge the power of God.

In order to do this you must put on a new pair of glasses. You must put on the type of glasses that will allow a person to see there are no coincidences, only miracles we just won't allow ourselves to see.

Take the next 60 seconds, that's all, pen in hand, and list all those things you are grateful for—Those things you are accustomed to having, or doing or getting; things that if they were not there your life would be different. I'll start the list for you.

I can: see, hear, walk, _____

_____

_____

_____

_____

I: got up this morning on my own without help._____

I:_____

I:_____

I:_____

I:_____

Prayer

Dear God:

I want to be in fit spiritual condition.

Empower me to trust in you.

Let me, daily, with each breath that I take, believe in you.

Help me to fine-tune my awareness of the miracles that continuously come before, actually preface, the one I am waiting for.

Strengthen me to live in the given moment; and, to find a miracle in each of those moments.

Bless me to know that when I take a breath that the circulation of the oxygen throughout my body is a bonafide miracle.

Let me never take for granted my ability to function mentally and physically, as I am accustomed to.

You have given me the capacity to do many things perhaps to walk, to talk, to hear, to feel, to see.

Grant me the grace to be in awe of this fact throughout each given day.

And God, don't let me take these powers for granted, doing them as second nature, but instead, let me do all you let me do in a mindful way—singing continuous and conscious praise to you.

Affirmations

- I trust in God.

- I believe in God.

- I want to trust in me. I want to believe in me.

- God answers my prayers.

- I know God, who is my Higher Power, is right here with me.

- A miracle is happening right now.

- Health, happiness, and wholeness is mine.

- I can heal, I accept God's healing; I am healing right now.

- God is the solution to all my problems.
  God, is right here with me right now.

- I call on God and God answers me.

- God is supplying me with every person place and thing I need.

- I know what to do and I am willing to do it, one step at a time, one thing at a time, believing in God all the way.

- I believe in God's everlasting love.

- I feel the Presence of God.

- God's light is my beacon. This light, of God, is guiding me.

Suggestions For Healing

Remember to Breathe

Make a conscious decision to choose to remember to breathe. Visualize God's Spirit within you. As you breathe in, feel the Spirit of God entering into every part of your existence. Throughout the day let taking the opportunity to sit still for a moment and breathe be an activity you consciously select to do. Actually let breathing be an activity of prayer.

Embrace all thoughts that enter your mind—embrace them and then embrace God

When a fear-based thought enters your mind (*I'm going to die; he will never get better, etc.*) embrace it and immediately embrace God, your Higher Power. Refrain from pretending that the negative thought isn't there or saying to yourself: "I shouldn't think like that, where is my faith?" Instead, when the fearful or defeated thought enters your mind acknowledge the thought, embrace the thought. And then, immediately say: I embrace God. God's all encompassing love is filling every inch of my being. God's love is filling my mind, my heart, my soul, my spirit, every cell in my body.

Byron Katie, in her book entitled *Loving What is*, says: "It's not the thought that hurts us; it is our attachment to the thought that causes us pain, that causes us trouble."

She advises one to call a negative thought a lie, to say to one's self: "Is that true? Could that possibly be true?" And then, to answer, no.

I agree with this. Anything, that contradicts the Truth of God's love, the Truth, that we will always be taken care of, no matter what the circumstances we find ourself in, is indeed a lie.

Get the facts

To make a decision, you need information. Find those persons who have studied the dynamics of your situation, whatever it may be, and based on their findings and your value system make a decision. Remember to take along someone from your support network to actually look for this data and/or to listen for you. Do this, just in case; just in case you start to experience feelings at a level that affect your ability to think and process the information.

Cry but never give up

Illness or any major life-changing event can be scary.

> If the
> burning of the brine-of-the-tears
> *well up* in your organs of vision
> flush them out.
> Let God's own
> *Spring-of-Freshwater*
> dilute the salt of pain,
> let the tears flow.

And, remember…God is with you!

FIVE

Another...Chapter
Another...Promise

SOME afflictions are so injurious that we can't bear to remember them. Remembered or not, sickness, untreated, has a profound effect on our day-to-day functioning. Just because I "forgot" I broke my leg 20 years ago, in no way negates the fact that it happened. I can limp along for years, behaving as though the way in which *I walk* is natural and healthy. However, my ability to move about unencumbered, the fluidity in which I can perform daily tasks, is profoundly impacted—each step that I take.

When these conditions exist, can I run the relay race untethered?

I think not.

Can I scale to the heights of the mountaintop without repeatedly falling and bruising myself many many unnecessary times?

No.

What does occur is that I limp along in various ways.

One way is at breakneck speeds. A manner many times associated with persons described as Type A personalities. Those folk who are said to be task and accomplishment driven; always on the go; impatient; quick-tempered; forever doing 5, 6, or even more things at once; most often "running" from one appointment to the next; and, rushing to meet deadlines. The list can, and does, go on and on.

Another limping along way is demonstrated by inertia or listlessness. This is the way usually associated with people who are described as depressed personalities—those folks who find it difficult to get in action;

are described as passive or indifferent; seem to do things in a half-hearted manner, with no enthusiasm; are languid; and, perform tasks in a perfunctory manner, doing "just enough to get by."

Many times folks in the Type A and the depressed groups have weight problems and eating disorders such as compulsive overeating, bulimia and/or anorexia. They very often have drug and/or alcohol problems.

The leg is broken. We don't know it. We try as best as we can to "run the race." Using whatever means we can to keep us in movement, or, to at the very least, prop us up.

In this chapter we will talk about healing from hurts so profound, that we might not have a conscious awareness of their existence.

With God's help, we will journey through exercises that are designed: to give us an awareness of the presence of old wounds; to help us to develop an acceptance of, what is — (acceptance that *this really did happen*); to question, actually ask God: "What is it, that *you* would have me do, so I can heal? *What actions, dear Lord do I take to heal?;* " and, to help us to follow through.

This is what is referred to in the 12 Step Programs as the three A's: awareness, acceptance, and action.

It is then, at this point, after having engaged in activities to heighten our awareness, our acceptance, and our ability to take action, that we are made ready for (ready to receive) the one true ointment of healing: the elixir of God's own healing love.

Sunshine...and, yellow flowers

"Sarah? Thank God! Please come and get the kids for me. I can't breathe. They're playing in the back yard. I don't want them to see me like this. They'll get scared. No, I don't need you to take me. I called a cab. I called my doctor. I'm going to the emergency room."

"Get her hooked-up to an I.V. What's her heart rate? Did those x-ray come down yet? Try to relax, now, Hanna. It's going to be all right. You're going to feel a little stick, but after that, you should start to feel a little better."

Lights everywhere. Movement: fast, hurried, a blur of bodies, colors, jostling, gurney by the wall, gurney jet-propelled down the hallway, gurney in a three-way, cloth-walled room, (*"Should I be hearing such intimate information about someone I don't even know? Hey, who are you over there on the other side of that curtain? At least tell me your name!*) Here we go again, gurney on air. Is this the hallway again? *What* could all the rushing be about? Hum, that feels good, nice and cool. *Sign my name? Oh, okay. Where?* Opps, rollie-polie, (*How'd they do that?*) better be careful, gon slide off the bed, gon fall between here and there."

"Come on, to the count of three; one, two, three, Let's go! Slide her onto the bed. Careful. Good. Now pull the sides up. Check the I.V. The drip still steady? Get her a new admit kit. Who's the nurse on duty? Doctor Garyotous will be in later."

"Hanna, you did real well, your doctor will be in shortly, your nurse is Dana."

And, with that, came the beginning of the rest of her life. An epiphany of sorts in that a kind of awareness began to creep in, flowering an understanding. It was, at once, and yet slowly, an *Aha!*, an, *Oh my God!* Three weeks in a hospital, that prompted, the end of a life as it had been known.

"Hanna, you know you really do need to slow down. That asthma attack you had, was so massive, you could have had a heart attack. Wanting to do better in life is a good thing. However, when you go at the pace you have been it has a damaging effect not only on your physical health, but on your mental and emotional well-being as well. I can give you another prescription, but a real change can only come about through some drastic changes, on your part, in life-style. Are you willing to do that? Your children, especially being as small as they are, truly need a mother there for them. And I'm afraid if you don't change, you won't be around for them as they get older."

She listened: quietly, intently, and when the doctor left, the tears came.

Several days of situationally forced reflection time brought about a confusing edginess. And, although there was someone awake and at the ready to make sure she was safe 24 hours of the day, some unknown, slightly sensed, danger, lay lurking just on the peripheral of her consciousness. It was a good thing she was in the hospital, because when the nightmares began, they were debilitating.

It would be months out of the hospital, several prescriptions of the powerful antidepressants Elavil and Prozac, as well as an admonition from Dr. Garyotous that perhaps she should see a therapist, before she was able to ask herself the question: *"What, am I afraid of?"*

Three years later, in her prayer groups, at A.A. meetings and in the support groups for survivors of all types of childhood neglect and abuse she could be heard saying: "And, it was for *that reason* (a deep-seated fear of remembering all of the childhood abuse, *the sexual abuse*) that I was in motion 26 hours of the day; took aspirin, tranquilizers, antacids, diet pills; drank beer (every night) to settle my nerves; worked too many hours; took too many college courses; parented my children alone; always had to have my house spotless."

She continued—"And, it was also for *that reason* that rather than participating in a graduation ceremony from college, as I had been scheduled to do on that day, that instead, I ended up in the hospital and spent three weeks of my life almost totally debilitated. I was without strength. I felt broken."

And as Hanna went on, one could see the pain, as she shared— "During the time prior to the hospitalization I could be found, on some nights, and many wee-hours of the morning, sitting in a catatonic state on the side of my bed, or on the sofa, or at the kitchen table, or sitting in a chair at the side of the bed of one of my two small children. Wanting to move, to get in gear, but not having the energy to hold my head up."

E'-li, la'-ma sa-bach' -tha-ni?

That is to Say: My God, my God, why hast thou forsaken me?

(Mt. 27:46 KJV)

Fear is a most devastating and incapacitating state of being. And, the unconscious goal to run from that which we fear can be the inducement for many life choices that will ensure that the dreaded awful hidden situation never gets a chance to appear on a conscious level.

This woman had no idea that the motivation for her constant seeking of a "better life," for herself and her children was actually a very creative way by which to keep the memories, which eventually surfaced, from springing forth.

She had no idea she had been sexually abused as a child.

She had no conscious memory of being molested by relatives and friends of the family.

When certain smells disturbed her, she dismissed it. When she, for no reason, would suddenly feel scared, she would shake it off — and "get busy." When someone would innocently pull a prank on her that she would go into a rage over, she had no conscious idea that the prank was reminding her of the secretive way in which the abusers of her childhood would lurk in the shadows and hurt her. She didn't know, for instance, that the reason she didn't like to have someone hold her wrist, no matter how gently, was because this was where the abusers would take hold of her and drag her to unremembered and unthinkable abuse; refusing to let her go.

What was the turning point for this woman? When was it that she was able to emotionally grab hold of God's hand and make the commitment to open up old wounds, to look inside, to let herself *see* what was actually " in there"?

It came, as she was going home from that hospital stay.

Still not able to drive her car, she sat in the back of a cab, window slightly ajar — the warm, twinged-with-cool-air breeze of the Chicago lakefront wafting through the vehicle. The sun seemed to dance, to skip across the surface of the lake — jetting, a high leg jig, akin to that of an Irish Riverdancer. And on her lap, sat a potted plant of yellow Mums, drawing to itself, and her, the healing rays of the sun. She wasn't consciously aware of the total healing effect of that moment, all she knew was the world looked different. Like something wonderful had happened to it during those long nights and days when the only thing that caressed her skin had been sanitized, chilling, unresponsive, hospital sheets.

Where are *you* on this continuum? Is there perhaps "something that is driving you" to suppress it?

Or, on the other hand, is there something so awful for you to remember that you are using up all of your energy to keep it buried? (And, it does not have to be sexual abuse; there are all kinds of abuse, all kinds of trauma.)

What is *your motive* for being in constant motion, or on the other hand sitting on the side of the bed unable to move?

Do you have some reason other than being a good person for always being the one your child's school can (and constantly does) call on for help? Are you the one who gets the job done, many jobs, over and over, at your church or is repeatedly being asked to be on this committee or that committee in community organizations?

Or are you at the opposite end of that spectrum: you do nothing; no one ask anything of you; you work, just barely; your house is a mess; your kids get on your nerves; you almost can't stand the sight of your mate. In other words—the house is bad, the job is bad, the mate is bad, the kids are bad; everything is bad! And, you don't have a clue as to why this is so.

And what about these things? Are you a stickler for always having everything in its place in your home?

Do you seem to "butt-heads" with people, a lot? For example: do your children, spouse, other relatives, friends, co-workers, or employees most often (according to them) have to "do it your way"?

Are you one of those well-intentioned people who takes control of situations that you see need fixing?

When you see a person in need do you jump right in there and make it all better for them, all by yourself, without being asked?

How good are you at letting situations resolve themselves, by themselves?

Think about it. To be a helper, one of good spirit, charitable, are fine attributes. However, if we use being a "do gooder" as a convenient smoke-screen to keep us from seeing our own needs for healing then we are doing ourselves a disservice. And, in the long run, we are actually doing harm to those we would help. The reason being: how can we be of real service to others if our motives are not truly based in love but instead are based in fear?

Whether you find it difficult to sit still, or feel as though concrete has been poured into and is lodged in your conduits of movement, God is there *right where you are.*

> Note: Prior to beginning the exercises in this chapter I want you to think about and then identify someone who could be there for you as you follow the instructions on healing. It could be a trusted friend, a prayer partner, a mentor, your sponsor, someone in your 12 Step Group whom you have heard share in meetings about healing from old wounds, or perhaps your minister. I want you to give them a call and say something similar to this: *I'm going to be doing some work that might involve opening up old wounds. Can I put your name and number in my book so I can call on you if I need support? And please, pray for me. Pray that I will keep in mind that I am worth doing this work and that I am worth doing whatever it takes to truly heal.*
>
> If none of these folk already exist in your world and you are pretty much isolated, then I fervently recommend that you look in the Yellow Pages and find the telephone numbers for the 24 hour Crisis or Cope Line in your city, several battered women's shelters, and your local YWCA. These sources would have a list of counselors, support groups, and agencies that can be of support to you. Many of the counselors and agencies they can refer you to will offer free, as well as a sliding scale of fees for services. Ask them for the name of a counselor you could contact about working with you. You could say: *I'm going to be doing some work that might involve opening up old wounds. And I want someone to be there for me. Can you refer me to someone who could help me through this process?*

Take a deep breath. Blow it out. Good. You can do this. Keep breathing.

Healing

True healing comes from God. God has the original surgeon's hands that can excise a wound, laying it bare so that the elixir of God's own healing love (grace) can flow through it and truly heal it.

Emotional wounds, similar to her sister physical wounds, over time can seem to heal. A covering, a skin, can seem to graft itself over the injury. However, the hide of denial lacks the ability to extract the pus that lays germinating just beneath the surface. To heal, one must take on a willingness, no matter how frail, to open-up and lay bare the hurts. We must, as it were, let God pour the peroxide of love into the open-wound so the infection can bubble up and out.

Raw?

Yes, raw, and sometimes in this process we will hurt.

However, God's own tender hand will be there to hold us, to comfort us. *Slowly releasing us* from the past trauma, hurt, and despair.

I invite you to take God's hand, and go on a journey of prayer and meditation, that will lead you to a healing. Take a deep breath now, take God's hand, and begin your activities to heal.

Activity:

Pray

Pray as though your life depended on it. It does. Pray in the morning. Pray at night. Pray all during the day. As we learned how to do in Chapter 4, take prayer breaks instead of coffee breaks. These breaks will sustain you in such a way that you will never feel the let-down that you get when the caffeine wears off after a coffee break. Your prayer can be as sophisticated as a long chanting mantra or as simple as saying the name of *your* Guiding Light: God. Jesus. Allah. Healer. Savior. Truth. It really doesn't matter how you pray, just pray. What you are doing, in all forms of petitions full of gratitude, as St. Paul talks about in the Bible, in his letter to the Philippians, is asking God each and every day in each and every way, for the grace to walk *this* journey of healing.

I want you to sit still for a moment. Did you do it? If you did, you just prayed. Congratulations! Now take a deep breath. Blow it out. You just prayed again. Visualize God's healing light flowing from the top of your head to the bottom of your feet. Allow yourself to feel the warm glow of God's healing touch. Again, you just prayed.

Look out of your window. Find a blade of grass, a tree, a flower, a twig, a patch of dirt, a child playing, someone walking by or driving by. Keep your gaze fixed on that object and observe what you have found for a moment. See the object or person, as is, God's creation. You just prayed.

Be gentle and kind to yourself. Yep, you just prayed again — one of the best forms of prayers in the world.

Lend a helping hand to someone. You just prayed.

Take a nap. You just prayed.

Wash the dishes, slowly, with gratitude that you are able to performed the task. You are praying.

Say no. No to overextending yourself. You just prayed.

Smile. You just prayed.

Laugh. You just prayed.

Say: I am mad. That hurt me. You just prayed. (We will discuss in more detail the expression of anger as prayer later on in this chapter.) But for now, just know that each time you acknowledge feeling angry, or feeling mad, while continuing to protect and look after yourself rather than hurt yourself or some one else, you are praying. And remember, as you go about doing what is recommended, prayer *is the foundation* to each activity you will engage in to heal from the past hurt.

Activity:

Validate — Make Real — What Is Going On With You

At various times you may find that you are scared for no obvious reason. This may occur when you are at home alone, in your car, or at work during a lull in activities. Perhaps certain sounds, noises, smells, situations, words, or scenes you observe on T.V. or in public places such as restaurants will spur a feeling of uneasiness. You might be super-vigilant, wary, on guard, super watchful, self-possessed, or over cautious. And one of the results of this wariness is you find it difficult to go to sleep at night, or your rest is fitful and you find yourself jarring awake throughout the night. At these times you may start to feel an eerie sort of fear. When this occurs do what therapists recommend, "validate the feeling."

One of the best ways to do this is to say to yourself: *I am feeling scared.* Even if you find it difficult to state this, or are not sure if the feeling you are experiencing is fear, allow yourself to acknowledge that what you are experiencing "just might be fear." And as soon as you acknowledge feeling scared, say to yourself: That was then and this is now. Whatever I might be feeling scared about right now happened in the past. I am safe now.

It is _____ and I can keep myself safe.

    (Put in the current date here)

I lived through whatever it was that is making me feel uneasy, and therefore I can live through the memory of what happened to me.

As you say this, I want you to do what Thich Nhat Hanh a Buddhist monk and Zen master refers to as watching your breath. I want you to consciously breathe in and out. Taking air into your nose, breathing it out through your mouth. With each breath that you take, I want you to watch that breath travel through your system. Watch it travel throughout your entire being. See if you can get yourself to visualize the breath entering the top of your head, traveling down your body, extending into your tummy, on down into your lower extremities until it reaches the ball of your feet. Then see if you can get yourself to imagine that the air is coming up through the bottom of your feet, traveling up through your legs into your tummy into your diaphragm all the way up to the top of your head. Let the breath that you take cleanse all that it touches (physical and spiritual) as it travels in and out of your body.

Activity:

Create A Support List

On the following lines write down the names of persons who you have come to feel good about. Folk whom you feel you could possibly call on to be of support to you. Someone who has shown in the past by their behavior that they are sturdy individuals with a sensitive and caring nature: A relative. A friend. A professional you have called on for advice. A member of your church. A member of a group you visited. A member of a group you are already a part of. Someone who is walking the same healing journey as yourself; since that person(s) is going through it also they will be a wonderful source of support and understanding. For those folk you are considering who are nonprofessionals, you want a person whom you have witnessed in the past standing by someone going through a trying time: A person who stood by that man or woman in such a way that the man or woman going through the challenge experienced this person as a buffer, a concrete support, for them if and when they needed it.

You'll want a list of names of a minimum of six persons who can be there for you at various times of the day or night. When you seek out the support of the folks to be on this list you want to find someone who is an early bird who arises at 4 or 5:00a.m., or a night owl who stays up until 10 or 11.00 p.m. You'll want someone who works the night shift-11:00 p.m. to 7:00 a.m., or midnight to 8:00 a.m. who would have access to, and permission to use, the telephone throughout the night. You'd be surprised at how many different wake/sleep styles people have. Query the folk you would put on your support list. Ask them: When would be the best time for me to call you? Are you a night owl, an early bird? Do you work at night? Can I call you during the night?

What you are seeking to do is to create a list of persons who can be there for you if and when you want or need support any time of the day or night. And, you want to create this list now, before you need it. Strategically place copies of your list wherever you might be so you can *just reach for it* if and when you need support. You can put a copy on the nightstand, in your purse/wallet, on the refrigerator, and in the bathroom.

You can do this. I know you can! Take a deep breath. Blow it out. Practice the breathing exercises as you learned how to do in chapter 1. Allow yourself to become centered in God. Pray. Ask God to show you how to do this and to empower you to follow through. Keep breathing!

Names:	Telephone #'s	Best Times To Call

Activity:

Call On Your Support People

It is very important that you give yourself permission to actually call on the people you have identified on this list to be of support to you. Many people who have been hurt in the past find it difficult to reach out for help. This is understandable. You were hurt in the past. Those who most often were responsible for taking care of you hurt you. Trust is violated when this happens. And many times when a person has been hurt as a child, when they reach adulthood they find it difficult if not impossible to trust another to be of help to them. In addition to this, many times the victims of past abuse believe themselves not worthy of the help of another. This could or could not be true for you. However, whatever your circumstance I want you to make it a priority to reach out to the people on your support list. This is especially important if you hesitate to reach out. If you find yourself saying something similar to: "It's okay. It's not that bad. I can take care of this. I don't need to bother him/her with this. This is silly. She/he will think I'm crazy. That's stupid. I'm a grown man/woman I'm suppose to be able to deal with my life." That's the time to reach out; pick up the phone and call. And remember: You can do this. I know you can!

Take a deep breath. Blow it out. Practice your breathing exercises. Allow yourself to become centered in God. Pray. Ask God to show you how to uncover the hidden and to empower you to follow through. You can do this!

Activity:

Choose Someone To Support You While You Search

At this junction of your journey to heal it would be good to seek out those professionals who have been trained to help someone who has experienced some type of past trauma. Remember, it doesn't have to be sexual abuse as the woman in the vignette eventually had memories of. It can be any type of past hurt that you have repressed the memory of having occurred. To do this, choose someone from your log of persons on your support list. Pray about it. Take a deep breath. Center yourself in God. And then, pick up the telephone and call several people.

Say to them: "I am going to be seeking out someone trained to work with persons who have experienced some kind of trauma in the past. I would like for you to be of support to me while I do this. I am going to be making telephone calls as well as going to interview different therapists. Will you be able to be of support to me in following through on these activities? If they say yes, then let them know you will be calling on them to schedule various times with them so they can be with you as you do what is outlined in the next two activities. I *encourage you* to do what is outlined in the next two activities. I want you to embrace and hold secure within your heart, that you don't have to do this alone. Allow the people you identified on your support list to actually be there for you, physically as well as emotionally and spiritually, as you take each step toward healing. That's why it is called support. Keep breathing!

Activity:

Find The Professional, Someone Trained To Help

There are many people in your community who know what you are going through, are trained to help you, are willing to help you, and are waiting for the call to be of assistance to you. I want you to believe this. Many of these people do this type of work because they too have experienced what you are *now* going through. And once they recovered, they made a commitment to reach out to those persons still suffering. They do this as a means of giving thanks for all they have received. It is now up to you to seek out those persons. This is where those people on your support list can be of great service to you.

I want you to take out the Yellow Pages again and look under counselors, Human Services Organizations, Social Services Organizations, Social Workers, Therapists, Volunteers of America. If you have access to the Internet you can go online and get this information.

If you find it difficult to follow through on this activity, do the footwork in stages. For example: On Monday you could give yourself permission to just look up and jot down in a spiral notebook the names and numbers of the various agencies. On Tuesday you could give yourself permission to pick up the telephone. You don't have to dial the number just pick up the phone. Wednesday just dial the number; you don't have to talk, just dial the number. On Thursday you could give yourself permission to stay on the line after you dial the number and when the person on the other end says hello you could then hang up. On Friday you could give yourself permission to dial the number, wait until someone answers and say hello. After you say hello if you feel uncomfortable you can hang up. If you feel relatively free from anxiety, able to ask a few questions, then stay on the line and ask to speak with someone trained to work with a person who is working on issues caused by trauma experienced in the past.

Healing from past abuse/hurts can be terrifying, so I want you to be gentle and nurturing toward yourself. On each step along the way to healing, *allow* yourself to do the suggested activities never force yourself. The abuse you lived through was forced upon you; do just the opposite as you act upon the suggested activities. So—*allow* yourself, invite yourself, Encourage yourself—to do that which God would have you do to heal.

And as you take the various steps to heal, remember to breathe.

Activity:

Interview Several Therapists

Once you have gone through the process of giving yourself permission to call and ask for help and you have secured the names, telephone numbers, and addresses of several therapists it then becomes time for you to interview the therapists and/or counselors you have found. Once again, this is where the person(s) from your support list can be of great service to you. You will want to take someone along with you as you interview each therapist. The process takes no more than 30 minutes. You will have a set of questions outlined for you later in this chapter. Your goal is to determine if you feel comfortable with the therapist. There are all types of therapists, and the fact that the person has been trained to work with someone who has experienced some type of past trauma/abuse in no way means you will automatically feel comfortable with that person. We each have very distinct personalities, therapists included, and each therapist has a preferred therapeutic style—a preferred way of approaching and dealing with past abuse issues. You want to be very sure that the person you select to help you has a manner of working that is in agreement with the way you best work on issues.

A word of caution here: I do not mean you will not feel uncomfortable at some point in the therapeutic process. What I mean is, for example, if you are a person who learns best when you are told about a subject, then going to a therapist that uses the inquiry method, asking questions, so you will "discover" the answer would most often not be a good fit. It's called chemistry. Does the therapist's personality go along with your personality? That is one of the factors that you will be trying to determine.

Another factor to determine is the therapist's belief system regarding the memories of a person who has experienced past trauma. If the therapist hesitates when you ask if he/she believes what a person says, or qualifies her/his belief, then in my opinion it would be better to keep looking until you have found someone who can say unequivocally: "Yes, I believe my clients when they tell me about what they remember, even if it is a vague memory of what has happened to them in the past."

Ellen Bass and Laura Davis in their book, *The Courage To Heal*, talk a great deal about the importance of having the person that you tell believe what you say is true. Bass and Davis tell us about the impact this has on the recovery process. They say it is vital that any person working with you believe to be true what has happened to you in the past.

Activity:

Select A Therapist

Once your fact-finding mission has been completed, to the best of your ability, take a deep breath and select a therapist. After you have selected a therapist, I suggest you make a six-week commitment for therapeutic sessions. I want you to continue to go for your scheduled appointments each and every week for the entire six-week period. Enter into a contract with God, your Higher Power, *That* which you hold to be sacred and yourself. In this contract, you will be making a commitment to do what you need to do, "One Day At A Time," for a six-week period.

Once the first six weeks are up you can at that time develop a Plan For Living on a month-to-month basis. At the end of each month sit down with those you have chosen to travel this journey of healing with and evaluate your level of wellness, your level of health, your level of being in *Fit-Spiritual-Condition*. Here are some questions to ask yourself: Are you where you want to be? Are there issues that still need to be addressed? Are you able to function on a day-to-day basis in the way in which you want to? Does it appear that you still need the support of a trained therapist to uncover, open-up, and heal old wounds? Once you have made this determination then chart your monthly course of action based on the facts that this weighing and measuring has revealed.

Activity:

Follow The Recommended Path Of Recovery

Throughout the course of treatment your therapist will recommend certain activities as well as literature designed to enhance and move along your healing process. The therapist may recommend that you join a therapeutic group where you can work on past abuse issues in a group setting rather than just individually as well as a support group for survivors. A trained counselor will facilitate both of these groups.

Let's talk about mindsets, now. It may be unsettling to think about going into a group of strangers and talking about things that are so disturbing that you can't remember some of it. Let me assure you that what you will get will far outweigh any discomfort you now feel thinking about it.

Once again I remind you that you can do this. Call on the people on your support list; enlist their aid just as you did when you were looking for a therapist. Ask several people on the list to drive you as you go about investigating the various groups. Learn to say to yourself, often: "As long as it is legal and moral, I am going to seriously take into consideration each and everything my therapist recommends. And, to the best of my ability, follow through."

Make a commitment to do your best. Praise yourself for each and every attempt to heal. Refuse to beat-up on yourself if your attempt to complete a task falls short of your expectations. And remember, the theme is "slowly and gently". Bit by bit, little by little, in a very nurturing manner (I repeat. In a very nurturing manner) follow the recommended path of recovery as outlined by the professionals, healthy survivors you will meet, and books on the subject of healing that you will read.

Activity:

Acknowledge that you just might be mad about the past hurt/abuse. Give yourself permission to get in touch with your anger. Learn how to get in touch with your anger. Learn how to get mad. Get mad. Express your anger in a healthy manner.

Ellen Bass and Laura Davis in their book, *The Courage to Heal*, tell us that anger is the backbone of healing: a transformative, powerful, healthy, reply to violation.

Most therapeutic works on how to heal emphasize the importance of the healthy expression of anger. We get mad as a natural response to pain, loss, grief, and out-of-control chaotic situations.

What is abuse, other than a painful out-of-control situation that leaves us grieving over the many things that have been taken from us — (losses.) Many of us have lost our virginity, never having given our permission for this to have happened. And, many times, it happened at such an early age that the memory of the occurrence defied our belief system. We also lost: usual (expected) healthy childhood experiences; expressions of nourishing, wholesome, parental love; images of good parents/caretakers — *decent, moral, respectable, upright*; a sense of positive self-worth; our innocence; and, our childhood.

We have been scorned for just being alive. Slapped, punched, pinched, beat, kicked, and burned. We have had food, proper clothing, shelter, and needed medical attention withheld from us. We have been yelled at, screamed at and told repeatedly through word and deed of our lack of value and worth. We have been locked in rooms, closets, and left there for hours and days on end. We have had our busted/split open, bruised, and swollen bodies put into alcohol laden scalding water and told it was for our own good.

Getting in touch with, and expressing your anger might be difficult for you. If it is, I want you to do something we have done before as we have traveled this journey of healing. I want you to do what is called *let's pretend*. In let's pretend, we pretend we are angry, mad, sad, etc. We step back and distance ourselves at least one step, from the situation and pretend it is someone else who is "getting mad, etc." This allows us to remove ourselves, something we were not able to do when we were hurt. By doing this, we are then able to participate in the activity without being suffocated by the experience.

We are now going to discuss some ways in which you can get in touch with, acknowledge, and express in a healthy way—as a form of prayer— your anger.

1. Become your own ally. To do that, it is important to get to know you, really know you. Those who have studied about and care about us being healthy, happy, and fulfilled human beings tell us there are many aspects to the human condition. Most folk can identify with what is most often referred to as the adult self. That part of self that goes to work, pays the rent, etc. Then, there is the part most often referred to as the child within: The part of us that is vulnerable. That part of self that seeks protection. The part of self that knows our history. The part that endured all of the neglect and abuse. And was, (remember this!) tenacious enough to suffer all of the abuse and make a decision to live anyway. To live, so you could come to be. If it had not been for that beautiful courageous child making a decision that she/he would live you would not be here on today. Applaud that child. Say thank you. And, make a conscious decision, as an adult, to: get to know her, make friends with him, listen to her, protect him, validate her outrage at having been hurt, embrace him and what happened to him rather than shun him and the memories of the abuse, and provide opportunities on a regular basis for her to express in a healthy way her outrage at having been hurt.

2. Make appointments to express your anger. Put that appointment on your schedule of daily prayer that you created. A good way in which to support you to regularly schedule times to express your anger is to structure the sessions for safety. One way in which you can do this is by jotting down on paper those things that surface in your conscious mind at various times that you are, or it is appropriate to be, mad about. Keep a mad journal. A journal specifically designed to "contain" your anger.

Throughout our day thoughts can come to mind that will trigger an anger response. It might be an inappropriate time to express the anger. — (You might be at work, with friends or with your children, etc.) If you have a place to *put the anger*, a journal for instance, then you can validate the presence of the anger, and go on with what you are doing. Then, at a later scheduled time you can release in a healthy way those feelings of anger.

Another good safety factor is to set a time limit on these sessions to express anger. To help you with this get some type of timer device — stopwatch, egg timer, etc. Then at the regularly scheduled time take out your journal. Set the timer for 2, 3, 4, or 5 minutes. You be the judge of how long. Just make certain to stay within a timeframe that allows enough time to "get it out" without causing you to feel like you will never return from that rage-filled place. If you stay too long, this then becomes abusive to you.

During these anger sessions you can use various techniques to healthily express your anger. You could, for example:

• Use the two-chair method: Arrange two chairs facing each other. You sit in one. Imagine that your abuser is sitting in the other. Take out your anger journal. Say: **I am mad at you because**: <u>read from your list of hurts</u>. Scream and yell at your abuser. Really tear into and blast that person. It is now safe to tell him or her off. Let that person have it. It is safe. *Keep breathing. God is with you.* You have a right to be mad. You have a right to confront them and their behavior. Remember it is energizing and healing to direct your anger where it belongs, at those who hurt you. If you don't you could very well misdirect that anger toward yourself and cause all types of problems such as depression. It would be good for you to remember that depression has been defined as anger and hatred turned inside, turned on one's self. Redirect that anger where it belongs and you will be amazed at how the headaches, backaches, and lack of energy will subside. Expression of anger is an absolute antidote for depression.

Keep breathing. God is with you.

- Stomp around the room. Take your list of hurts in hand and stomp all around the room that you are having your session in. Scream and yell at the abuser(s) as you read what is on your list. **I'M MAD AT YOU BECAUSE YOU**: <u>read from your list of hurts</u>. This is a very good exercise because it allows you to release all sorts of pent in rage and hate in a very physical way. It has also been successfully used with small children to allow them to healthily express feelings of being mad about something.

Keep breathing. God is with you.

- Take a big, red plastic bat, the kind children use when they are playing ball. Get some pillows. Stack them up in a pile. Place your anger journal where you can read it without holding it. Take the bat in both hands and while reading from your anger journal start beating the pillows with as much force as you can while you scream and yell at the abuser(s) **I'M MAD AT YOU BECAUSE YOU**: <u>read from your list of hurts</u>.

Keep breathing. God is with you.

- Buy a punching bag. Install the bag in a room that can be used for your anger sessions. As you punch the bag visualize the person(s) who abused you. Beat that bag as hard as you can. All the while telling that person off. Learn to scream and yell and release that pent up rage. **YOU HAD NO RIGHT TO DO THAT TO ME. I HATE YOU!** (It's okay to say I hate you to your abuser.) **I HATE WHAT YOU DID TO ME. I DESERVED BETTER THAN THAT! I DESERVED TO BE TREATED WITH RESPECT. I DESERVED TO BE NURTURED. I DESERVED TO BE CARED FOR!**

Keep breathing. God is with you.

- Save old newspapers. Put a pile together and when you get mad sit in your safe room and tear paper up as you blast the abuser for all of the hurts inflicted upon you.

Keep breathing. God is with you.

- Schedule anger sessions with your therapist. Call someone from your support list who has shown that he/she can handle the expression of strong feelings. Take your anger journal out and lambaste your abuser while your therapist or friend keeps safe, the parameters of the session—(you, the timeframe, what you do during the session, etc.).

Keep breathing. God is with you.

- And most especially, Remember the Rule.
  The rule is: To Be Safe. Safety At All Times.
  No hurting ever, of your self or any other person. And, the next part of this rule is, once you have opened up and expressed your anger make sure to get closure. To get closure, you wrap up the session. Never leave yourself open, raw, from any activity you engage in to open up old wounds. It is equally as important, some say more important, to end a session in a healthy way as it is to open up the old wound in the first place. So think open and close. Wrap yourself up in healing, nurturing activities designed to bring you back to the here and now. Tired, perhaps, but in complete possession of your faculties. Thinking: I am an adult. Today is _____. I am safe. That was then. This is now. I am healed. I am safe.

Once you have gotten in touch with the process of anger—(how to open and close a session), and have learned to befriend all parts of your self and have made a commitment to routinely express, in a healthy way, your anger, as a form of prayer, you could—(without actually being in the same room with this person)—confront your abuser.

Here is an example of how you can go about doing that. Gather around yourself your support team (your therapist, someone from your list of support people, etc.). Tell them: you are ready to spiritually (not physically) confront your abuser; you will be looking back at what the perpetrator did to you; you will be writing down what the perpetrator did to you; and, you will be confronting (on paper and in your safe place—the therapist office, your living room, etc.) the perpetrator. Ask your support people to pray for you and then proceed to do the following.

Gather up your writing materials — (pen, pencil, writing pad). Go to that safe place that you have identified within your home. Position yourself comfortably in a chair, with something to write on — (a desk, this book, a sturdy cover on the notepad, etc.). Take a deep breath. Blow it out. Do this several times. Center & Ground yourself in God. Talk to God: *Dear God: You and me — Together…Can do this. You Leading & Guiding me. Me following. Take me where I need to go to heal. I place my faith and my trust in you, Oh Lord. Where you Lead I will go.* Breathe in and out deeply, wholly, and fully. Then, look back. Allow yourself to remember a little girl, a little boy. Innocent. Eager. Pure of spirit and of heart. Open, welcoming, seeking love and affection. Can you see her? Can you see him? Good. Now, allow yourself to remember, actually visualize, one of the most hurtful, unexpected experiences that child endured.

Keep breathing. God is with you.

Write that occurrence down on the following lines or in your writing pad. Write what the perpetrator did to that *beautiful, Innocent. Eager. Pure of spirit and of heart. Open, welcoming, seeking love and affection* child. Write down what that innocent child went through.

Keep breathing. God is with you.

You can do this! Keep breathing.

Take a deep breath. Keep breathing. God is with you. You are safe.

As soon as you have down on paper what the perpetrator did to you, immediately put it aside (in a safe place). Breathe in fully and deeply. Say God's name—Jesus. Allah. Immanuel. As you breath in, actually allow yourself to feel(to breathe in) the sustaining healing power of God. And once done, call on your support team. Let them affirm and reassure you— (pray with and for you). After you and your support person have prayed together and you are centered and grounded in the *Here & Now* (the day that it is) schedule a time when you can meet with this person to spiritually (not physically) confront the perpetrator.

When you and your support person meet with each other you can confront the perpetrator in the following manner.

Allow yourself to go back to the place that you wrote about when that beautiful child was abused. But this time you will go to that place in a different manner. You will go back with God. You will spiritually go back with God as well as you the Adult person as the Protector of that *beautiful, Innocent. Eager. Pure of spirit and of heart. Open, welcoming, seeking love and affection* child. With God as your Guide, Helper and Protector you will *Spiritually go back* and be the Powerful Protector of the child you once were. — *Towering* over the abusers of that child. Take what you wrote about, what the perpetrator did to that beautiful child. Read out loud what the perpetrator did to that beautiful child. Scream at the perpetrator for hurting that child. Tell them to:

**STOP THAT! GET YOUR HANDS OFF OF THAT
CHILD! LEAVE THAT CHILD ALONE! THAT IS
A PURE AND PRECIOUS CHILD!
A CHILD WORTHY OF BEING NURTURED
AND CARED FOR!
GET YOUR HANDS OFF OF THAT CHILD!**

Scream at the perpetrator. Let the perpetrator know how you feel about what he or she "is doing" to that child.

With the help of God and your support person scream and yell at the perpetrator until you have let out and let go all that has been held in and pent up and pent in for years.

Have your support person, the one who is physically there with you in the room, monitor and structure the session for safety. Tell your support person to cue you for safety, to quietly tell you throughout the confrontation (when needed) things such as: *Breathe. You are safe. Step back. Keep breathing. That's enough.* — (This is especially important if perhaps you go too far in the confrontation such as trying to continue to scream and no sound is coming forth). You want the confrontation to be a cathartic experience. — Healing and cleansing *void* of all injurious behaviors being displayed by yourself upon yourself.

Remember, anger — getting mad, is the backbone of healing. It is transformative, powerful, and healthy. It (anger), expressed in a healthy way, is prayer.

Keep breathing. God is with you.
I'm proud of you!
You are worth healing!

Activity:

Create A Plan of Healing, A Plan For Living

You will develop many plans for living. At the beginning of the journey you will have one sort of plan. In the middle of the journey, at various points along the way, you will have other types of plans for healing. And, at the end of the journey (yes, there will be an end to this process) you will have a different type of plan for living. During one of your *sit down and be quiet and feel the Presence of God* prayer times I want you to create a plan of safety. The following is designed to help you create this plan of healing. Which, in essence, is your Plan of Safety, your Plan For Living.

When I begin to feel uncomfortable, scared, anxious, fidgety, mad, or any other feeling that is stopping me from enjoying the moment I will:
  • Acknowledge that the feeling is real rather than try to suppress it. And then, let it surface
  • Pray
  • Remember to keep breathing.

- Cry when I need to.
- Scream and yell when I need to. I will immediately schedule an anger session. Always remembering the safe parameters of an anger session—I open it up and I close it up. And during that session I will scream and yell and direct my anger where it belongs, at my abuser(s).
- Call someone on my support list.
- Tell someone on my list, a trusted person, what I remembered.
- Rely on others, especially those, who have already walked the journey I currently walk and are now healed.

Personalize your list. Put things on it that have had a restorative effect upon you in the past.

_____

_____

_____

_____

_____

_____

_____

_____

In your plan of safety you will want to include a daily way of taking care of yourself. A human being does not experience feeling scared, mad, etc 100% of the time. Sometimes we feel just ordinary. But even when we feel just ordinary, we want to have a schedule of activities designed to help us to enjoy the day and to feel safe and secure. Each of us needs to take care of our mental, physical, emotional and spiritual well-being.

On the following lines put one activity that will provide for your wellness in each of these states. For example:

Mental — read something to improve my mind.
Physical — Do stretch exercises. Or, jog in place. Or, walk.
Emotional — Call someone on my support list. Share my feelings.
Spiritual — Pray at 6:00 a.m, 12 noon & 9:00 p.m.
All of the above: *mental, physical, spiritual, and emotional.* — Practice my breathing exercises. Regularly schedule and participate in anger sessions.

Personalize your list. Put on it those things that have, in the past, enhanced your physical, mental, emotional, and spiritual well-being.

Mental _____

Physical _____

Emotional _____

Spiritual _____

All Of The Above (*mental, physical, emotional, spiritual*) _____

_____

You will also want to include in your Plan For Living what I refer to as a contingency plan, an emergency plan for those times when the pain of the journey can seem more than we can bear.

This is what I want you to do:

Make a list of those things, those activities, that you enjoyed doing before you began this sometimes painful journey of healing from past trauma and abuse. Keep this list in a spiral notebook along with the names and telephone numbers of your support team. Make a duplicate copy (2 or 3 copies if needed) of this notebook. Keep these notebooks in specific places where you can easily put your hands on one if and when you need it. And, after any painful experience, nurture yourself by participating in something you have put on your list. What you want is to do things that have brought comfort to you in the past and will, most likely, bring you comfort again. Here are some examples of activities that could be on your list:

- Look at old Perry Mason Movies.
- Take a slow leisurely walk.
- Play with your cat or dog.
- Hug a stuffed toy.
- Drink herb tea or warm milk.
- Bake cookies.
- Play your favorite music and sing or hum.
- Do crossword puzzles.
- Do yoga stretches.
- Exercise.
- Dance.

Personalize your list. Put on it those things that have, in the past, brought you comfort.

_____

_____

_____

_____

_____

_____

_____

_____

Prayer

You, oh Lord, are my Higher Power. And, I need a healing.
I sit in prayer asking for guidance and direction.
I don't know if I can do this, but I am going to try.
I don't know if I am hiding anything from myself, but I know
I'm tired:

- Tired of trying to fix things;
- Tired of rushing around;
- Tired of hurting;
- Tired of dragging around;
- Tired of trying to find, each and every day,
  the energy I need to do the things I need to do;
- Tired of eating too much;
- Tired of not eating enough;
- Tired of stuffing myself with food and then
  forcing myself to vomit;
- Tired of drinking alcohol;
- Tired of using tranquilizers;
- Tired of using other drugs;
- Tired of being mad, at the world;
- Tired of being pushed around;
- *Sick* & tired of being sick and tired;
- Tired of waiting for it all to be alright.

I turn over to you my needs. I sit to the best of my ability,
listening for your directions on the best route to take to heal. I
ask for the willingness to hear "the Truth." And God, when it
feels as though I just can't make it, I just can't bear up under it
anymore, help me to remember that pain has a beginning and an
end. And that because I have *You* on the journey I will be
protected. And, *I will survive.*

Affirmations

- God is Here.

- Together, God and I can handle anything that I remember.

- With each breath that I take I am being protected.

- I am worth healing. I can heal. Wellness is my birthright.

- Breathing in, I breathe in God. Breathing out, I let go fear.

- I survived whatever happened to me; I will survive having the memory of what happened to me.

- I am healed. I want to be healed. I am healing. I am worth healing. God is healing me.

- Together, God and I can handle everything that happens today.

- I choose life. I choose Grace. I chose a life of healing.

- I Trust God. I trust me.

- I believe in me. I believe my memories.

- I seek a Higher Power, one greater than mine. I seek God.

- I put my faith, my hope, and my trust in God.

- God and I are partners.

- I trust God. I believe in God. I trust me. I believe in me.

- I feel the healing Touch of God.

Suggestions For Healing

Remember to Breathe

Very often when we are anxious or agitated (highly emotional), especially if it is on a subconscious level, we inadvertently hold our breath. Make it a point to do what is called: Watch your breath. That is, make a conscious effort to track your breathing pattern. Example: Breathe in through your nose. Smile. Slightly part your lips. Hold that breath for a slight moment. Release the collected air through your slightly parted lips; through that smile. Repeat this several times, until you experience being relatively centered and grounded in God. Watch how your chest lifts up and out as you breathe in. Then watch how your chest concaves in (drops down) as you release the breath. You can know that you are breathing correctly if you are breathing as an infant does while sleeping on its back. Think about it, the infant's chest and tummy goes up and down in a smooth, gliding motion. If you would like to, you could add the following affirmation to your breathing routine: *Breathing in I quiet my mind, my heart, and every cell in my body. Breathing out I let go tension.* The important thing is to remember to breathe. This, (breathing) is a form of prayer.

Believe That You Can Heal. Create An Environment For Healing

Surround yourself with a condition of healing. This includes your mindset, your living conditions, and your associates. You want to hold close to yourself people who believe you can heal, people who have healed, and people who know how to and can direct and support the healing process. The way in which you carry out daily assignments is also important. You want, to the best of your ability, to implement tasks in a way that is as free from pressure as possible. What you are looking to do throughout the day is to support the process of healing.

To develop the mindset that you can heal, remind yourself over and over that you can heal. Silent as well as audible affirmations simply stated will help to change your mindset from one of victim to survivor. Look at the previous affirmations and select one or two favorites then say them throughout the day. And the standards—*I am healed. I want to be healed. I am healing. I am worth healing*—all are good basic affirmations.

Affirm and reaffirm your ability to be safe

Opening up and facing old hurts can be scary. Each of us has a basic need to know that we will survive. Reminding ourselves that we are safe and will remain safe is an important component of the healing process. We will repress hurtful memories because we fear that we won't survive the hurt that we are remembering. Reminding ourselves that it is just the memory of what happened not the actual injury will help us to continue doing what we need to do to heal. Say to yourself: *I survived what happened to me, I will survive experiencing,* having, *the memory of what happened to me.*

Let it be okay, good in fact, to call on someone for support

We can stop the healing process by being resistant to reaching out to those who can, and are willing to, be of support to us. When thoughts of *she's too busy; he doesn't care; she'll think I'm weak; what would they think of me; I can handle this; I'm supposed to be able to handle things like this, it's only a feeling!; it's not that bad* invade your mind, reject those thoughts. Stop yourself from succumbing to them. These thoughts stop us from moving ahead in our quest for healing. When thoughts such as these surface, acknowledge them. Say: "I'm thinking like that again." And then immediately tell yourself: "Those thoughts will stop me from healing." As you say these words call on God (your Higher Power) to help you to reach out to the person God *wants* to be of support to you. Keep your list of names and telephone numbers where you can put your hands on it without much thought—in a place, where you can "just reach out for them" during those times when you need to hear a calming, reassuring, supportive voice. Have a copy wherever you might be at any given time of the day or night.

Memories, when we give them permission to surface, have no special day or time to make themselves known. I have had memories of past abuse while sitting in a restaurant eating a carrot salad. The salad along with the sight of a little girl having dinner alone with her dad sparked a memory that had been buried 25 years!

Remember, you are worth healing. There are people out there willing, wanting, to be of support to you in this journey. And besides, think of all the people you can reach *your* hand out to, once *you* have healed. God bless; go for it!

Remind yourself (frequently) that pain has a beginning and pain has an end.

At the moment that we are experiencing any type of pain we can tend to forget that it will stop at some point. The fear, that it will last forever, actually has the effect of prolonging the pain. And, as a result, our minds shut down to the healing process; our muscles tense up even further; our hearts race; we stop breathing correctly; and we get caught up in a web of pain that could be described as a low-grade, subconscious panic attack. When this happens, say: "This will end soon. Pain has a beginning, pain has an <u>end</u>!" Then, watch your breath, make a conscious attempt to smoothly breath in and out, calling on God (your Higher Power) with each breath that you take.

Trust your instincts, trust your memory: trust that the hurt is real

To heal from hidden wounds we must take on the mind-set that: It did happen. Certain memories can be so traumatic we will want to reject them. We will want to say: "That didn't happen. That couldn't have happened!" When this occurs, say: "God, help me! This is awful. This is <u>real</u>!" If you are able to, write it down. Get a journal. Keep it in a safe place and, as soon as possible after having a memory, write down what you remembered. Writing down what you remember has two primary benefits, one is that by writing it down you *publish it*, you make it real. And the other, is that you stop yourself from re-repressing the memory. Left to memory (*I'll remember that*), the awful hidden act will very often retreat into the walls of our subconscious mind. Take care to keep in mind, that it is important that you trust that it is real; that you acknowledge the hurt; that you write it down; that you reach out; and, that you call someone.

You can heal.

You *are* worth healing.

Affirm You. Trust You. Believe Your Memories.

Tell yourself that you are telling the truth when you have a memory. Tell yourself that you are worth helping. Tell yourself that the pain is real. And therefore, it makes sense that you would feel hurt. Give yourself permission to feel the pain. And then, call on someone. Call on someone on your support list, because this pain <u>must</u> be addressed.

Be gentle and loving with yourself.

Never force yourself to do anything. Allow yourself to remember that as a child you were forced to do many things. This is one of the ways in which you were abused. Therefore, choose to do just the opposite in your healing process. Give yourself permission to do the various recommended activities. *Choose.*

Remember Your Worth

You are worth each and every step recommended for you to take to heal from past trauma and abuse. Keep this thought uppermost in your mind. Keep it as an affirmation. When the road gets tough, say to yourself: *I am worth it. I can heal. A state of healing is my birthright.*

Use Anger As An Activity Of Prayer. Let it be okay, good in fact, to get in touch with the experience of being mad about having been hurt.

Every activity that we participate in can be an activity of prayer. Many times people who have been profoundly hurt as a child will misrepresent anger as something to be avoided. This is understandable. Anger was maligned. Anger was used as a weapon. I want you to change your mindset about anger. I want you to think of anger as healing, energizing: an emotion, to build with, rather than tear down with.

If someone steps on your foot it's okay to say: Ouch! If someone slaps your face, causing your head to jerk around, leaving the crimson sting of violence implanted on your cheek, it is again okay, good in fact, to say Stop! And, let the heat of anger rise to the surface, revitalizing you, as you say: Halt. Stop that. Get away from me.

Someone stepped on your foot, on purpose. It hurt. You didn't do anything to cause that person to do what they did. You were, and are, a good person. You deserved better treatment than that. Think about it, if someone offended or intentionally hurt someone dear to you, you would get mad about that; right? Yes, you would. Well, someone dear to you—you—did get hurt. And, it wasn't (believe this! It wasn't) your fault. Get mad!

Reach Out For Help When You Need It

Never discount a painful feeling. If you feel uncomfortable call someone.

Journal

As an act of faith, as often as possible—daily, every other day, weekly—allow yourself to sit quietly and listen. And as you "listen," jot down what you hear. For example, if the thought of a doctor, therapist, minister, trusted friend, 12 Step or support group comes to your mind, jot that down. If you start to feel scared, no matter how subtle, jot that down. If you feel nervous, jot that down. If a scene from an old occurrence in your life surfaces, jot that down. Refrain from analyzing, or (especially) rejecting any thought that comes into your mind. Just allow yourself to *be the recorder* of the information that surfaces.

In A.A. there is a affirmation that goes like this: God and I *together* can handle anything that happens. For our purposes here on today, let's retool that saying and declare: Together, God and I can handle anything that I remember. Quietly repeat this affirmation throughout each day. And remember, journaling is an act of prayer and meditation. God will, if you allow Him/Her, place the thoughts that you need into your mind. Think of journaling as just a session where you sit and talk to God, your primary Therapist, and you jot down the conversation on paper.

QUESTIONS TO ASK
THE VARIOUS THERAPISTS

• Have you been trained to work with persons who have experienced past abuse? And if so, what did that training consist of: where, how long, with whom?

• Have you ever worked with someone who has been or suspects they have been abused? And if so, how long have you worked with persons suspected of being abused as a child?

• Tell me your thoughts about the memories a person has of past incidents of abuse.

• Do you believe what your clients tell you when they share with you their memories of incidents of being abused as a child/infant?

• What method(s) do you use to help a person unlock stored memories; open up old wounds; acknowledge that what they remember is real; identify what hurts; develop plans of safety; develop plans of healing; develop plans of action?

• Do you use the discovery method or do you use a direct approach? Tell me, what can I expect when I work with you?

SIX

Another...Chapter
Another...Promise

WE develop many patterns of behavior on an unconscious level. Some social scientists suggest that as children we do this, most often, through a series of play activities where we act out behaviors we have observed others displaying. And, Alfred Adler, a respected, and much quoted social scientist, held that it was *this* (modeled behavior) rather than any other avenue of learning that humans acquire the rhyme and rhythm of social order.

Think about it. Small children at play routinely imitate the behaviors of adults. They will wash the dishes, mop the floor, play dress-up, teach the class, be a student, put on make-up, shave, dress the baby, chastise the child, fuss at the baby, spank the baby, "so he will be good."

Be good! You be good now!

One only has to look at the facial expressions of these children and observe the intense levels of concentration they display to get an understanding of the depth of their involvement as they take on the role of an older person in their life and portray that individual's behavior.

In this chapter we will discuss patterns of behavior and how they are learned, but more importantly how they can be unlearned. Activities are provided that have been designed to heighten one's awareness. These activities have been fashioned in such a way as to help us uncover current mindsets as well as reveal the type, scope, and the *actual effect* of our present day behaviors.

Strange lodger, Caged...

"Get your stupid ass, in here!"

And it would start once again.

"Didn't you here me? I said: **Get your stupid ass in here!**"

Marsha fidgeted, confused about what to do, wanting to run, but glued to the spot. If she did as requested, she was *sure to get* whacked. If she ran she was *sure to get* brutally beaten.

"No, Ma, I didn't do that!"

"Stop lying to me. Yes you did go into my perfume. Look at it. It's all cloudy where you put water in it so I wouldn't know you had been in it. How many times have I told you to stay out of my things? You did too do it; **Stop lying to me, you little Bitch!**"

"I didn't mean to...

The screams were bloodcurdling.

"**I'll show you how to lie to me!** (whack) **Shut up!** (whack) **Didn't you hear me? I said to shut up!**"(whack)

Her eye was swollen this time. The tee shirt, bright yellow smiling face on the front, lay crimson red, stuck to the welts that lay criss-cross down her back.

Scared that "those people" would start looking for Marsha, the mother called the school.

"Marsha got a cold. Tell her teacher. She'll be back to school in a day or two."

In fact, what actually occurred, was that Marsha was out of school two weeks this time. The swelling around her eye and the blood stained cornea seemed to "take forever," to clear up this time. The welts across her back, as in the past could be covered over with a thick, oversized sweater. And although the welts was the more serious of the two injuries, it was the eye that kept Marsha out of school. "Too many questions. Too many prying people" would be the rationalizing thoughts tumbling through the mother's head as she daily, made the decision, to keep Marsha home from school once again.

"Why can't those nosey busy-bodies mind their own business?!"

"Spare the rod, spoil the child. God knows this child has been spoiled enough. That's why she gets into so much trouble. That's why she's always touching everything and getting into God-knows-what! And I try, God knows I try hard, hard as I can, to get her to be the child I *know* God wants her to be! Those nosey busybodies! Why can't they mind their own business!"

"I'm sorry Mrs. Motley but you will have to have a written doctor's order for Marsha to return to school. It is the policy of the school system that any child who is absent over three days must have a doctor's slip to return to school."

"I fell. I was running and fell down."

This was the response, over and over; each time the doctor questioned one of the old, not so old, and new bruise marks that tattooed Marsha's body.

"The bond is set at $200,000.00 dollars."

"But we don't have that kinda money."

The judge repeated himself. "The bond is set at $200,000.00 dollars. The defendant shall remain reclused until such time as bond is paid." And with that, the bang of his gavel resonated throughout the courtroom like a chime, bouncing from place to place, corner to corner. "Next case!"

It would be several days, almost two weeks in jail, thinking she was going to "lose her mind," before the mother struck on an idea on how to get out. She mortgaged her home and got $20,000.00, the 10% of the bond she needed to get out on bail.

"It is the order of this court that the minor child, Marsha Grisham, biological child of Dis'ray Motley, be allowed to continue to be domiciled at 2246 Ruston the home of the biological mother but be placed in the custodial care of the maternal aunt Jennifer Jans, who will also reside at said residence. It is also ordered that the agency known as Child Protection continue it's involvement in this case and that qualified staff from this agency complete a thorough investigation of this matter. It is then ordered that daily unannounced visits be made to the home to ensure that the child is being cared for in the manner in which the court decrees. The mother, Mrs. Motley, and the child, given name Marsha shall each continue to receive crisis therapeutic intervention followed up by ongoing therapy sessions. If, at any time, the child's welfare is in question she shall be immediately removed and placed in the court's custody. Is this understood?"

"Yes Your Honor."

And the journey from abusive parent began.

Through the investigation it was found that Marsha had been repeatedly beaten. Overtime, as the inquiry proceeded, Marsha was able to describe incidences that indicated she had lost consciousness during many of those beatings. Through the doctor's examination it was discovered that Marsha had many old wounds. The initial impact of these wounds had been so brutal that the wound should have been treated by a physician. And one of the lacerations had been so severe that a plastic surgeon needed to and should have been called in.

Marsha was a wounded child, inside and out. Her gentleness of manner belied the violence she had lived with. Bright, intelligent, eager to please are just some of the adjectives the social workers used in their reports to describe her. It defied logic that this child had been so routinely and severely beaten that she would involuntarily flinch when the social worker would lift her arm, pen in hand, to make any kind of innocuous move.

Months and months went by: "But I can't!"

"Yes, you can."

"No, it's impossible. I'll never be able to make it right."

"To stay in the past will only hurt Marsha more."

"How can you say that?'

"Easily, I have talked with your daughter. She is ready, more than ready, to move on, to live in the present, and to let go of the hurt and pain. It is up to *you* to help her to do that; to live in today; and, to make each day a safe day."

The mother went through much court-ordered and then self-initiated treatment. It would be years before she was able to connect the abuse she had withstood as a child with the abuse she had inflicted upon her young, innocent daughter.

Many guttural primordial screams had to be unleashed before she was able to release the anguish of her own childhood: Being shackled inside a cage, like an animal, naked, and left in an overgrown country backyard.

Months of treatment would pass before she was able to acknowledge what she had subconsciously rationalized, for years: *"But I'm not putting her in a cage. She got her clothes on. I don't starve her. I let her stay in the house. I fix her scars up. I give her a hug when I'm through being mad."*

Breaking the chains of abuse, Dis'ray Motley, the mother—the *tragedy* of modeled, and then learned, persecution—from the pain of jail, from the hell of hidden affliction, bursting forth into awareness...came, promise.

For us, humankind, our first avenue of instruction is what we see, observe, hear, and then feel. No one need tell us that *this is the way it is*. We see it repeatedly being done to ourselves or others and we instinctively take on the notion that this is the way it is supposed to be. Whether it be putting on our shoes, hugging another tot, playing house, pretending to hold a baby, we learn how to do this from what we see and observe. It stands to reason, then, that abusive behavior (when it is adopted as a form of behaving) would also be learned in this manner. I am beat, so therefore I beat. I am screamed at, so therefore I scream at. I am pushed, shoved and degraded, so therefore I push, shove and degrade.

What did you learn as a child? What types of behaviors were modeled for you? They need not be as severe as the ones this mother learned. But think back. Are there any behaviors you observed and then adopted, whether in a subtle or blatant manner, that need to be erased? What are you modeling for your children? How do you treat those close to you? Are the use of scalding humiliating words the way in which you get *your* point across? Do you find fault before you voice a compliment? Is there most often a "yes, but" attached to the positive comments that you begrudgingly give?—(*Did I do the dishes like you wanted them Ma? Yes, but, you could have done the stove better. Dad, I finished washing the car. How'd you like it? It's okay, but you could have done the tires better.*).

There are many ways to contribute to the destruction of another person's sense of positive self-worth. And most of these forms of wreckage are subtle. But the result is the same; they destroy a person's sense of value.

Is this what we want? Do we really want to tear apart the heart of another, to annihilate the core of their goodness? I don't think so. Even the convicted murderers I have worked with have expressed a sense of remorse over deeds done out of fear-based rage.

How can we be sure that we are building up, rather than tearing down?

We can allow ourselves to develop an understanding of what we are actually doing; not let ourselves stay locked into what our intentions are, but instead get a clear picture of behaviors being displayed; and, let ourselves see how, in fact, our actions (what we are doing) affect another.

The following activities have been designed to develop this type of insight.

Activity:

Awareness

Try to imagine that I am sitting there with you. Or, if you would rather, imagine a trusted, non-critical friend or mentor sitting there with you. It really doesn't matter, who you choose, because in actuality it will be God there with you. You've merely put a cathedral around the Holy Spirit—what a trusted friend of mine refers to as "God with skin on"—when you allow (or imagine) a trusted friend to physically be there in support of you.

Now that you have mentally called on someone to be of support to you, I want you to think about something. Many times we paint the picture to color it in the way we want it to be rather than how it actually is. The mother in the story colored her picture to reflect a good mother endeavoring to teach her child right from wrong and how to live on the straight and narrow, righteous course of life. The mother took on the position that if you spare the rod you spoil the child. However, she carried that belief way beyond the usual social and moral boundaries. Did she know she had swung the pendulum over far too wide? In all likelihood, no. What she wanted was for her daughter to be "a good child." But instead, the mother produced, and got, a beaten and broken of spirit little girl. And, a dirty little secret (what she was doing to her child) to boot.

Where does your behavior lie on the continuum of being the stimulus for that which you want? Are your behaviors actually yielding the desired results? Here is where the awareness comes in. Once again, as in the preceding chapters, I encourage you to take a compassionate look within.

Remember, let this look backward be, to the best of your ability, <u>void</u> of all judgment of you, all criticism of you. And, refrain from defending your actions or rationalizing your behaviors. When we start defending or rationalizing our behaviors we shut down the process of honest and open reflection. What you are endeavoring to do throughout this chapter is to get a clear picture of "how it looked."

God wants you and your loved ones healed. To heal a hurt we must first know what needs mending. The following activities give you a way to know.

You can do this! I'm praying for you and right along with you! *Breathe.*

A good way that I have found to accomplish this (the looking back) is to act as if you are observing the behavior of someone else.

Read the following questions.

After each question allow yourself to look back. Create in your mind a moving picture show of past behaviors displayed by you toward others. Without commentary, check off yes or no to each of the questions.

Is your manner toward your child ever one of scorn?
    Yes ___ No ___.

Do you ever look at her with a look of disgust on your face?
    Yes ___ No ___.

Is your message to that child ever one of: You don't do anything right. You just can't get it right?
    Yes ___ No ___.

Is your manner toward your child most often one of disapproval?
    Yes ___ No ___.

Has your manner ever been menacing?
    Yes ___ No ___.

Have you ever berated your child in manner or word?

Yes ___ No ___.

Have you ever screamed at your child?

Yes ___ No ___.

Have you lost your temper with your child?

Yes ___ No ___.

Have you said things to your child that were hurtful to him and the comments caused him to lower his head in shame?

Yes ___ No ___.

Have you ever hit your child?

Yes ___ No ___.

Have you ever hurt your child in another way?

Yes ___ No ___.

Have you ever let your child be hurt by someone else?

Yes ___ No ___.

Very good. You did well. Take a deep breath. Several cleansing breathes. Let God's love fill every inch of your being: your mind; your heart; your soul; your spirit; and, every cell in your body.

Ask God, your Higher Power, to guide you through this activity. Ask God, to remove any inclination to judge, criticize, defend, or rationalize your behavior.

What you are seeking to do is to develop an awareness of, as well as identify, behaviors displayed by you.

Take a few more cleansing breaths. It is a form of prayer. Sit quietly. Reflect on what you have just checked off. Now ask yourself if you can go on at this moment, or is it time to stop for today. Let God guide your answer. You will know from this place of prayer and grace what to do. When it is time, either today or at another sitting, for you to go forward I want you to proceed to the following activity.

Activity:

Insight

What you are looking for now is insight into the dynamics of your behavior. You want to know what has occurred when you have behaved in any manner that caused you to check "yes" to any of the previous questions. For example: When we look at our child with a look of scorn or disgust, that son or daughter can show signs of confusion, sadness, shame or fear. I want you to think back to one of those occasions when your child has lowered his or her head in what seemed like confusion, sadness, shame or fear. What happened just prior to you looking at your child in that manner? Write down what you remember. Take your time. You can do this.

_____

_____

_____

_____

Once again, take some cleansing breaths. Sit quietly. Reflect on the activity. Think about what you have just written down. One more time, ask God, your Higher Power, to fill every inch of your being. As you feel God's healing grace fill the space within you, release anything that would stop you from going forward. Say to yourself: *I can do this. God is near. God is here. God is present as I look back at my behavior.*

Can you go on, or is it time to stop for today? Let God guide you. Let God provide the answer. You will know, as I said before, from this place of prayer and grace what to do. When it is time (either today or at another sitting) for you to go forward, complete the following. You are still endeavoring to develop insight into your behavior.

There is an origin, originating point, for each action one takes.

Where do you think you giving your child the message you don't do anything right; you just can't get it right, comes from? What could cause your manner toward your child most often to be one of disapproval? Think about it. Where did you learn this behavior? Who did *you* see display this type of disapproving behavior? Pray. Ask God to open and direct the passageways of your memory. Write down what comes to mind.

Take a deep breath. Blow it out. You can do this.

_____

_____

_____

_____

_____

_____

Good. You did it. You're hanging in there. And once again, I remind you to take some cleansing breaths. Sit quietly. Reflect on the activity. Think about what you have just written down. Call on God. Ask God, your Higher Power, for the grace to continue. As you feel God's healing grace fill the space within you, release any pain you might be feeling. Say to yourself: *I can do this. God is near. God is here. God is present as I look back.* Now ask yourself if you can go on or is it time to stop for today. Let God guide your answer. You will know from this place of prayer and grace what to do. When it is time (either today or at another sitting) for you to continue moving forward, to unlock the doors of the past, I want you to address the following.

Menacing and Berating Behavior:

Think back to those times when you have screamed at your child and lost your temper. What was going on at the time? What happened just minutes before your outburst? Is this usual behavior for you in that you routinely "lose your temper" and find yourself screaming at your child? Who modeled screaming behavior for you? Was your household one of calmness when you were growing up or was it one of screaming, yelling and berating behaviors being displayed? If it was the latter, how did it make *you* feel when older persons screamed and yelled at—you?

Let yourself remember being yelled at.

Pray.

Take some more deep-cleansing breaths.

Write down what comes to mind.

You can do this. I know you can.

Hang in there. It's (you are) worth it.

_____

_____

_____

_____

_____

_____

Congratulations, you hung in there. Breathe. Sit quietly. Reflect on the activity. Think about what you have just written down. Call on God. Breathe. Ask God, your Higher Power, for the grace to continue. As you feel God's healing grace fill the spaces within you, release any pain you might be feeling. Say to yourself: *I can do this. God is near. God is here. God is present as I look back.* Now ask yourself if you can go on, or is it time to stop for today. Let God guide your answer. You will know from this place of prayer and grace what to do. When it is time (either today or at another sitting) for you to go forward, do the next activity.

Force. Blindness. Boundaries.

Have you ever hit your child? Have you ever hurt your child in another way? Have you ever let your child be hurt by someone else?

Read the questions. Think about each one. Pray for the grace to be steadfast, to remain present, to remember that which happened. And, to have the courage to state factually what occurred. Then, write down what comes to mind. Remember, you are not alone. God is right there with you. God knows what your intentions were. God also knows you want to be healed from that which is troubling you. Take a deep breath, a deep cleansing healing breath and begin.

Question:

When I have hit my child what happened just prior to me striking her? What had my child done?

What did I hope to have happen as a result of having hit my child?

Were there any bruises left on my child when I slapped, backhanded, kicked, whooped/beat, whacked, her? — (*No matter how small a bruise, list it.*). Was the skin ever broken? Was there ever any blood? — (*List even the slightest show of blood*). Were there ever any broken bones?

Did my child ever "get sick " after being hit by me?

Did my child ever stay home from school after being hit by me?

Did my child or I ever invent a story about a scar on her that was a result of being hit by me?

Have I ever been scared after hitting my child?

Have I ever had to say something similar to this after having hit my child?: "Well, she deserved it. If she wasn't always getting into so much stuff I wouldn't have to go that route. I wouldn't have to hit her. It's for her own good. I don't want her growing up wild. Anything could happen to her if she don't learn how to behave."

Allow yourself to recall as many instances of you hitting your child as possible. You are seeking, with God, your Higher Power's help, to open up the past. You want a clear picture. You want to know about the different settings, situations, and circumstances under which you have hit your child. Look at behaviors only. Refuse to criticize yourself or to rationalize your behavior. Stop yourself from explaining "why" you did what you did. Just write, on the following lines, what you remember happening. Write down the *what* happened rather than the *why* it happened. You can do this!

Keep breathing.

_____

_____

_____

_____

_____

_____

That, took courage. You are doing a good thing for both yourself and your child. I know this taking a close look at your behaviors without adding an explanation of why you did what you did might be scary, but keep at it. It will all be worth it in the end.

Once again, take some cleansing breaths. Sit quietly. Reflect on the activity. Think about what you have just written down. One more time, ask God, your Higher Power, to fill every inch of your being. As you feel God's healing grace fill the spaces within you, release, to the best of your ability, any pain that may be present. Say to yourself: *I can do this. God is near. God is here. God is present as I look back at my behavior.*

Now ask yourself if you can go on or is it time to stop for today. Let God guide your answer. You will know from this place of prayer and grace what to do. When it is time for you to go forward (either today or at another sitting) answer the next question.

Question:

Have I ever hurt my child in any other way? For example:

- Did I call my child names? What are the words I used?
- Did I pinch, shake, shove, or push my child?
- Did I restrict my child's movement in any way?
- Did I verbally threaten my child?
- Have I ever put my child on punishment for weeks or months at a time?
- Each time I get mad do I bring up things my child has done in the past and then add that to the list of what I am punishing her for?
- Have I ever bound or tied up my child?
- Have I used any type of object that has inflicted pain or bruised my child in some way?
- What does punishment from me look like?
- What are the things that I do when I punish my child?
- What are my methods?

Again I remind you, without judgment or criticism, answer the above questions.

_____

_____

_____

_____

_____

_____

_____

_____

Once again, take some cleansing breaths. Stay with me now. I know you can do this! Keep breathing. As you practice your breathing routine…Sit quietly. Reflect on the exercise. Think about what you have just written down. One more time, ask God, your Higher Power, to fill every inch of your being. As you feel God's healing grace fill the spaces within you, release any and all pain. Say to yourself: *I can do this. God is near. God is here. God is present as I look back at my behavior.*

Now ask yourself if you can go on or is it time to stop for today. Let God guide your answer. You will know from this place of prayer and grace what to do. When it is time (either today or at another sitting) for you to go forward answer the following question.

Question:

In what ways have I let my child get hurt by others? What are some of the behaviors I have displayed that have allowed my child to get hurt by others?

Allow yourself to pray and reflect on this question. You are seeking, with God's, your Higher Power's, help to open up the past. You want a clear picture. You want to know about the different settings, situations, and circumstances under which you have allowed your child to be hurt.

For example: We can turn over what we call discipline, but in actuality is punishment, of our child to another. We can let others abuse our child in some way. We can remain silent when we know our child is being hurt by someone. We can make excuses for the behavior of the person who is abusing our child. We can imply it is the child's fault if they are being hurt by another. We can try to convince our child that if he/she would somehow change their behavior the person abusing them would stop.

We can keep the secret, and persuade the child to keep the secret, when our child is being hurt by another. There are many subtle as well as blatantly open ways in which a child can be hurt. Gently and — as best as you can — lovingly, ask yourself: Have I ever let my child get verbally, emotionally, physically, or sexually abused? Have I ever let my child's boundaries be violated in some way? Remember, let this look back be, to the best of your ability, <u>void</u> of all judgment of you, all criticism of you.

And, refrain from defending your actions, or rationalizing your behaviors. When we start defending or rationalizing our behaviors we shut down the process of honest and open reflection. What you are endeavoring to do in this activity is to get a clear picture of "how it looked." Let God, your Higher Power, guide you. Take a deep breath. Several cleansing breaths. And, know (absolutely know) that God is with you. God wants you and your child healed.

To heal a hurt, we must first know what needs mending. This activity is a way to know.

You can do this!

I'm praying for you and right along with you!

Breathe.

_____

_____

_____

_____

Congratulations! That took courage! You hung in there! Once again take some cleansing breaths. Sit quietly. Reflect on the reason we are doing this, and that is…. **to break the chains that Bind us!**

Think about the things you wrote down. Pray. And, one more time, ask God, your Higher Power, to fill every inch of your being. As you feel God's healing grace fill the spaces within you, ask God for the grace to be able to release any pain you might be feeling. Say to yourself: *I can do this. God is near. God is here. God is present.*

Let's take a look at the word and the concept of courage. *Courage*— is defined as the ability to confront that which is feared. Using that definition, you indeed have courage, the courage to face and open up old wounds.

It has been said that behavior that hurts another is a wound of the past that one keeps re-enacting over and over and over again. Every time I scream at my son, it is *my father*, once again, towering over me, yelling…at me. And, I am in pain (once again) as my body and my mind and my emotions remember the assault. Each time I strike out in violence, *my wound, quivers.* It is as though my stepmother is once again putting me in that tub of scalding hot water...*for my own good.*

Yes, it has taken Courage for you to bring to light that which was hidden. And, it shall require the grace of God for you to remain steadfast. Your guarantee, God's Promise, is that you shall have what you need to continue this Journey. Believe it!

Lessons On Healing

Let us now take a look at how healing occurs.

In this chapter, you have uncovered behaviors displayed by you which have caused some form of pain. To stop this type of behavior, to have what you need, and to enjoy God's Promises, there are certain things you can do. The primary thing you can do is to learn a new way to behave.

Take a look at the following list. It addresses the behaviors we have focused on in this chapter: one's manner; looks of disgust; hidden messages; screaming-verbal assaults; physical harm; and, pain we have allowed to be inflicted upon our loved ones through other avenues. The list also contains the corresponding opposite behaviors that are designed to heal. A simple, but as mentioned before, *not easy* exercise, that is designed to heal old wounds — is to look at each behavior, and then, do just the opposite. Look at the following. It lists painful behaviors (which is the negative) versus healing behaviors (which is the positive).

Painful Behaviors (-)	Healing Behaviors (+)
Scorn.	High regard
Disgust	Value
You don't do anything right.	You truly try hard.
You just can't get it right.	You are so talented.
Disapproval	Approval & Admiration
Menacing	Comforting & Encouraging

Berate	Applaud. Pay tribute to
Scream. Yell	Speak softly.
Lost temper	Compassionate
Hurtful, shaming words	Words of endearment
Hit	Counsel with love & understanding
Violate boundaries.	Respect boundaries.
Passive abuse	Hands-on caretaking

This list, in its entirety, contains straightforward and uncomplicated behaviors. And that's a good thing. However, to heal we must take the list one step forward. The side that identifies the healing behaviors contains behaviors/responses that when put into daily practice will ensure that you automatically respond to your loved ones in a manner designed to heal you *and* them rather than continue the cycle of generational abuse that has been designed to hurt; to inflict some kind of pain.

Lesson on Healing: (1.)

You can turn scorn or disgust or any one of the painful behaviors listed, into a healing behavior such as—showing a manner of high regard or value, *by routinely practicing* the following:

- I will become a sentryman of my own behaviors. By daily, observing and watching, to the best of my ability, each and every response I have to another's words and/or behavior. I will *immediately acknowledge* that I am feeling or wanting to respond in one of the ways as listed under the painful behaviors.

- I will at once, without delay, call on God. I will pray: *Please help me! God, show me another way. Dear God, touch my heart and soul. Let me softly speak to and touch my child.*

- I will take a deep breath, several deep breaths. And, as I'm taking these deep breaths…

- I will physically remove myself from harm's way. I will take 3 steps backwards. I will put my hands in my pockets. I will turn and walk away. I will sit down, on my hands, preferably in a different room.

- I will say to myself: *Wait. Be quiet. Stop. Go into Time Out.*

- I will allow 5 minutes to pass <u>before</u> I say or do anything in response to something I got upset about. If, after 5 minutes, I am still upset I will let another 5 minutes pass, and another 5 minutes pass (and keep doing this) until I am calm and in control of my behavior, *prior to saying or doing anything in response to what I got upset about.*

- I will soften the edges of my mouth as well as my expression, and "act as if." *Act as if* I'm pleased with the person. *Act as if* I hold the person in high regard and value that person. *Act as if* that person has done it, whatever it is, just the way I wanted it done. *Act as if* I'm pleased. *Act as if* I admire the person and value his/her efforts. *Act as if* I approve of that person.

You are doing a great job! Let's keep going.

Lesson on Healing: (2.)

Remembering to always begin with those things you learned how to do in Lesson on Healing # 1, here are a few specific examples of ways in which you can substitute a healing positive behavior for a painful negative behavior:

<u>Disapproval</u>   V.   <u>Approval & Admiration</u>

Rather than waiting for my child to do something wrong and then showing some form of disapproving behavior. I will look for opportunities to "catch him being good." No matter how small or insignificant I think the positive behavior being displayed by my child is, I will point it out to my child and others. For example: *Wow. You sat there for one whole minute. I'm so proud of you. I only had to call you once this morning and you got up.*

Congratulations! Dad: did you see how well John is playing with his sister? Gladys, you got one more math problem correct this time on your test. Congratulations. Good job; your room looks real good! You got those dishes done before I came home. Way to go!

<u>Menacing</u>   V.   <u>Comforting & Encouraging</u>

The next time your child behaves in a manner that you would usually display a menacing manner to "get her back in line," do this instead. Say: "I understand that it is sometimes difficult to do all of the things we expect you to do. I can remember how hard it was for *me* when I was your age. I didn't do it all right all of the time either. But you know what, I would be willing to bet if you and I sat down together for 15 minutes each week, just you and me, we could help you help yourself to do those things we expect of you."

Here is another way in which you could approach this situation. You could say: "Come here." And then give your child an all-encompassing hug. A hug designed to dissolve the hurt and disappointment. We all need a hug when we fail to live up to expectations.

<u>Berate</u>   V.   <u>Applaud, Pay Tribute To</u>

Every week find one opportunity to applaud the accomplishments of your child. Look for a *glimmer* of the behavior you want your child to develop. Then write down the date and time that you saw your child displaying this behavior. Later that day, at lunch or at dinner, or after your mealtime, tell everyone in earshot about your child's success. — *Hey family Jada started her homework without me telling her to do it!*

<u>Scream, Yell</u>   V.   <u>Speak Softly</u>

Make your car or some other safe place your screaming, yelling place. When you feel as though you are going to act out and scream and yell at your child, do the suggested activities in Lesson on Healing # 1. Then go into a room other than the one your child is in and call someone. Tell them you are ready to blow your top. Tell them to talk you down. Then get in your car. Don't move it. Don't drive upset. Just get into your car and scream your head off: *How could you do that? How could you be so stupid? You knew better than that!* Say all those things that you would have screamed at your child. And remember, a zipped lip is one of the most important new skills to acquire when you are learning a new way to behave.

Say to yourself, often, "Keep your mouth closed." Words said out of frustration and anger cannot be retrieved. You can think a thought and change it. You can replace it with a healing, nurturing thought. But the spoken harsh word, even after an apology, cuts deep and leaves a wound that can sometimes take years to heal.

Lost Temper   V.   Compassionate

Things will occur that will prompt us to lose our temper. We are human and things are going to upset us. It is okay to get mad. It is *the way* in which we *express* our anger that rampages its way into the territory of abusive behavior on our part. Get in tune with your bodily reactions. Register what happens when you "get mad." Does your stomach get into a knot? Does your breathing get short? Do you get hot? Do you clench your fist or grit your teeth? How do you respond, when you are getting ready to lose your temper?

Once you are in tune to your bodily reactions to anger, use the time-out method; separate yourself from the source of your anger. If you are mad at your son, stay away from him for 5, 10, 15 minutes. (see Lesson #1) Do whatever you need to do to calm down. Refuse to go into a self-righteous mode: such as *How dare he!* Think back to when *you* made a mistake. Then speak softly and with understanding. Develop a plan of action designed to allow you to handle the offending situation in a gentle and concerned way.

Hurtful Shaming Words	V.	Words of Endearment

In a state of frustration we will inadvertently lash out at our child (or any loved one, for that matter) and say cruel and spiteful words that cut into the very core of that child's soul leaving a deep wound. The child will feel humiliated and mortified, sometimes taking on the mindset that he or she is dirty, refuse — not even worthy to be in the same room with "nice people." That child's self image and sense of self-worth can be crippled. To change that type of knee-jerk behavior, begin to practice saying words of endearment. Daily, even if it seems silly, look into a mirror and say these words: *I am glad* that — *you are you. God created you, and God, only creates the Best! You made a mistake? All of us humans make mistakes. Brush yourself off. Take a deep breath and let's try that again. I know you can learn how to do what you are trying to do. Believe in you: I do!*

Believe it or not, daily practicing the saying of these words or some similar affirming words will have several benefits. First, it will train your subconscious mind to reach for the endearing word. As you say these words, this Litany of affirming positive utterances, you are teaching your mind to supplant (unseat) the old and plant (set in place) the new. Then, when unsettling situations arise, rather than a humiliating word popping out, a positive word will come forth. Secondly, this practice in effect brings about, produces, the healing of two people, <u>you</u> and your child.

Hit	V.	Counsel With Love & Understanding

Hitting is another knee-jerk reaction. Some parents have used physical force for so long they automatically reach for the belt, slap, backhand, push or shove in response to some perceived infraction. When we hit our child we most often think it teaches them to "stop doing that!" That assumption has proven to be false. Studies of human behavior, done over generations, have established that to hit a child ultimately teaches them one thing, to be afraid of us. And in addition to this, fear — (as born out by the many murderers who continue to be placed on death row) — has not and does not act as a deterrent to undesirable behavior. This same research proved — (through the behaviors displayed by the people who were tracked, in some instances over a 40-year period) — that persons respond much more enthusiastically to praise and reward than to insult and punishment. We can begin to develop this skill of using praise and reward, through practice.

The following is one global illustration of how to go about acquiring this new skill. Daily — find, look for, the opportunity to counsel with love and understanding. For example: You are preparing breakfast. Your child walks into the room. While the two of you are in the same room, strike up a casual, "let's pretend" conversation. For instance, you could say: *"Let's pretend that this might happen today."*

In the conversation you will share with your child a healthy way to handle a situation that she might encounter in her day. Using as an example, a situation she previously experienced and it had turned out badly. You will not, hear me, will not, browbeat her or scold her in any form or fashion. Instead, you will in a casual conversational tone, give her step-by-step instructions on how to successfully handle the situation.

You could share with her ways to handle being teased by the other children. Or, you could give her instructions on how to manage being scolded by the teacher for not doing something the teacher wanted her to do. You could say something similar to this: "Jill, let's take a minute and think about the rest of the day. There are many things that can and will happen today. Yesterday (last week, etc.) was kind of rough for you. You (got into a fight, were suspended, didn't finish your homework assignment, didn't do your chores before I got home, fought with your sister, came home late, etc.) I *know* you didn't like how these things turned out. I *know* (in my heart) you want to make things better. I would like to help. Would you like for me to help? If you would, we can create a plan, together, that I believe can be of help." — [Note to you, the reader: We can't change everything about our behavior at once. So when you talk with your child, name one thing, <u>one situation only</u> that you might have gotten mad about. And because you wanted your daughter to change the behavior you resorted to physical force and hit her.]

If you, routinely, on a daily basis, work on one offending behavior at a time, you will garner the same results as the 40-year study: changed behavior on the part of your child.

Let's now take a look at some physical exercises that you can practice that will *help you* — change the knee-jerk reaction of hitting your child. I want you to daily, take the time to schedule, when you will actually sit on your hands. This won't take long. Here's how: Take a small notebook that will fit in your purse or pocket. Each morning, or the night before, write down four times within the day when you will take a timeout to practice "keeping your hands to yourself." I have found in working with parents who had routinely used physical force that just the simple act of scheduling a time to sit on their hands, to reflect on what they had done with their hands, and then vowing to do it differently — brought about miraculous changes in their own behavior. One other thing that has garnered much success has been to create a Plan-of-Action. Here is a suggested Plan-of-Action that has proven to be helpful for many parents.

Plan-of-Action

If and when I get the urge to hit my child I will:

- Acknowledge the thought/feeling.
- Take a deep breath, and while I am taking in that deep breath,
- Call on God: *Please help me! Keep me safe. Keep my child safe. Stop me! Stop me! Stop me! Heal me. Heal me. Heal me.*
- Immediately physically remove myself from the child.
- Call someone on my support list.
- Keep breathing.
- If, possible, go for a walk — get out of the house.
- Sit on my hands.
- Keep breathing.
- Keep praying throughout each activity in my Plan-of-Action.

Violate Boundaries   V.   Respect Boundaries

To violate a boundary means that I have in some form or fashion stepped over the line of what is appropriate healthy behavior into the territory of inappropriate behavior.

Inappropriate behavior includes calling names, verbal attacks, punishment for weeks on end, overt (blatant, out in the open) and/or covert (subtle, hidden from view) sexual abuse, restricting my child's egress (movement) in any way, as well as, any type of behavior displayed by me that caused my child some type of emotional pain.

Whatever you identify that you have done that has violated your child's boundaries in any "form or fashion," vow to do it differently. If you have, for example, identified that you:

- Call child names   Say the kind word
- Verbally assault   Affirm your child

(See previous sections in this chapter on screaming, yelling, losing temper etc)

- Punish child   Discipline child

(See Section Suggestions For Healing/Be Vigilant, at the end of this chapter for an example)

- Sexually abused   Seek help immediately.
  Respect the following boundaries. Never do anything that would cause you or your child to be stimulated sexually. Never walk around nude. Never stand in the doorway of the bathroom or the child's bedroom watching a child's private moments. Never call a child nicknames such as slut or whore. Never interfere in any way with what is (for most of us), the usual healthy progression of a (your) child's sexual development. (For additional healing alternatives to sexual abuse see Suggestions For Healing at the end of this chapter).

Passive Abuse   V.   Hands-on-Caretaking

A passive abuser is one who is aware of a child being abused but will stand by and fail to say anything or display any effective behavior that will stop the abuse. On the other (beneficial) hand, the person who uncompromisingly watches out for their child (a sentryman of themselves as well as others), will actively participate in the rearing/development of their child. For example: a hands-on parent will:

- Speak up when they become aware of their child being hurt in any way.

- Tell the offending person to Stop! And then report what was done to those persons (professionals) who can insure that the child will be kept safe. In so doing, the hands-on-caretaker is providing a way for the offending person to get help — (*if* he/she so chooses to accept this help) — to learn a new way to behave.

- Be the child's ally. And, let that child know it is not his/her fault that someone is hurting them; never, excusing nor glossing over an abuser's actions.

- In a forthright manner, place total responsibility for the abuse squarely where it belongs, with the abuser.

- Tell the secret. Help the child tell the secret. Keep the child safe, and be of support to the child while the abuse is brought out into the open.

- Stand up!, for the child. And in so doing, will:

  Protect that child from verbal, emotional, physical, and/or sexual abuse. Insisting, at all times, that the child's boundaries always be respected by all who come in contact with him or her.

Take a look at the following recommended affirmations. Say them. Let them become a part of who you are. Take them on, as your new underlying message. Let the words contained therein be that which rest in your subconscious mind. You were once taught to hate. Now learn, through changed behaviors —

Thoughts. Words. And, Deeds. — How to…Love.

Affirmations

- God loves me. God is with me. God is helping me.

- God is showing me another way. God is touching my heart and soul; showing me how to softly speak to and softly touch my child.

- I *can* learn a new way of behaving.

- I *can* learn a new way of speaking.

- I *can* learn to change what I believe is the right way to help my child and others.

- Each time I inhale, the love of God flows through my body

- Each time I exhale, the forgiveness of God is draining away every hurt of the past. I let go fear. I let go rage.

- God forgives. I want to forgive. I forgive myself for showing a lack of love.

- I let go of the past and embrace *this* moment; I embrace God.

- God has the solution to <u>all</u> my problems.

- Goodness comes from nurturing thoughts, words & deeds. There is power in good thoughts, words and deeds.

- Real love begins with me.

- When I display love toward me I can display love toward others.

- I can think the nurturing thought. I can say the nurturing word. I can do the nurturing thing.

- No matter what, God Loves me.

Suggestions For Healing

It is time for healing. It is time to soothe that still raw wound. Through these suggestions, grab hold of God's hand. You can do it. You can change. God says so!

Be vigilant. Refrain from ever glossing over or justifying, past behaviors and remain on guard concerning current behaviors.

1st: Learn to be a sentryman of your own behaviors. Stand guard over and be watchful of that which you do. Remain mindful of the fact that your behaviors are a product of that which you have learned. And, remember: just to make what you did more palatable to you, at any given moment you can fall prey to justifying and/or glossing over behaviors displayed by you in the past that have inflicted some type of hurt upon another. When we justify or gloss over there is a danger we will repeat the offending behavior. And, since behaviors are a learned skill, it is important that we acknowledge the facts of what actually occurred, and make a conscious decision to behave differently, to behave in a manner designed to heal rather than hurt.

2nd: You want to make sure that there is no hint of punishment in that which you do. It would be good for those of you who are still actively parenting children to learn the difference between punishment and discipline. The key to remember is punishment inflicts some kind of mental, emotional, or physical pain. Whereas, discipline offers a learning experience, some kind of instruction.

For example: A child comes home later than agreed upon. A form of punishment is that the parent will scream and yell at the child (somehow berating him in word and/or manner) about how bad he is for not coming in at the agreed upon time. The parent might even slap, push, or shove the child. That is considered punishment. On the other hand, if the mother duly notes that the child has come in later than agreed upon, and tells that child how disappointed she is and how scared she was when the child failed to show up at the agreed upon time, the child learns that others are affected by his/her behavior. Once this has been established, the mother could then tell the child that due to him coming in late he will have to cancel a date scheduled for the next day. The additional knowledge here is that the child learns he must come in at the agreed upon time or else experience the natural consequences for his behavior. In this case it would be he forfeited the privilege of going out for an upcoming activity.

Use The Past Only For Healing Instruction

When you begin to think the thoughts or to behave in the ways noted on the Painful Behaviors side of the comparisons list we have been discussing, ask yourself the question: Who, in my lifetime behaved toward *me* in that manner? Who, gave me the impression that I couldn't do it right? Who behaved toward me in a menacing, scream-in-your face way? Who, chose to hit *me* rather than take the time to speak and give healthy instructions? Whose painful behavior am I imitating?

Remain Open to learned information

As you walk this journey of discovery you will become aware of mindsets and behaviors that perhaps had been hidden from you. Some of these, which, upon close scrutiny, may seem repulsive to you. If or when this happens, stay put. Remain open to that which is revealed to you. Refuse to shut the door on this new information. If you allow yourself to remain present, to embrace that which is, to unlock the hidden, you will find after a while that some of the mindsets and behaviors you have closefistedly held onto, for many years, are no longer of service to you.

Learn to see the value in changing old behaviors

You can, if you allow yourself, learn to observe—you. When you do this, you will be able to see, in a clearer manner, your mindsets and behaviors. Once you have acquired the skill of looking at yourself in a nonjudgmental compassionate manner, you can then ask yourself the question: Is this mindset/behavior getting me what I want, or preventing me from getting what I want? If the answer is, yes, it is getting me what I want—a better lifestyle, changed behaviors on the part of others—then hold on to it. If the answer is, no, it is preventing me from getting what I want—then, it would be advisable to—Let It Go!

Develop an awareness of what to do to change.

To effectively *initiate* and *continue* the process of change a condition of personal safety must be maintained.

Personal safety entails the following:

Breathing.

Making a commitment to keep breathing no matter what.

Being nonjudgmental and non-critical.

Taking on a mindset that will allow you to be gentle with yourself.

Looking at behaviors only.

Seeing what you did (your behavior) as a mistake, a learned behavior, an error in judgment.

Repeatedly saying to yourself: *I did the best I could do, with what was modeled for me. I deserved a better model. I deserved better than that; my loved ones deserved and continue to deserve better than that from me. I now have an awareness of a different way to behave. I have the power to select a new way. I have the power to behave in a different way. I CHOOSE a new way. I CHOOSE to behave differently.*

Begin the process of Change

Be gentle with yourself. For change to occur we must give ourselves permission to change. The best way to do this is to face squarely those behaviors once displayed and perhaps are still being displayed and say to ourselves: this is either helping me or hurting me. Which is it? And, then to the best of our ability, gently and lovingly, step-by-step do a new thing.

Accept Responsibility For Behaviors & Move On

In health, we acknowledge what we did; accept responsibility for what we did; ask God, ourself, and the person we have harmed to forgive us; and, make a commitment to God and ourself to do it differently the next time. A note of caution here: Early on, in the healing and changing process, we do not want to make a verbal commitment to the person we have harmed because we might not be able to keep that promise and we would, in essence, compound the hurt. And, hurt them all over again. It is recommended that we do what is referred to in Alcoholics Anonymous as a "living amends." We vow, through our behavior, *one day at a time* to do it differently. And we do just that. Another point I'd like to make is—refuse to wallow in the pain of what you did or what you were thinking about doing. Instead, plant yourself firmly in the here-and-now of recovery. Step away from the pain. And, move on.

Ask for help—(Support)—Someone and something to help you make the needed changes

You are not alone. There are compassionate and loving people out there who understand what you are going through. They understand because they have been where you are. Once in their life, they too behaved in ways and manners they could not understand. And later, when they thought about those behaviors, they were repulsed by the memory of what they had done. If you have ever felt this way, then there are people out there *waiting* to be of support and assistance to you. But you have to muster-up the Courage to ask for that help.

You can do this. I know you can! Take a deep breath. Blow it out. Say: *I can do this. There are people who know what I am going through. There are people out there waiting for me to call on them so they can help me. I am a good person. I might have done things I am ashamed of, but I am a good person. Someone out there is waiting, to help me.*

Now pick up the phone and call one, some, or all of the following places.

People, places and things that can help you heal

PROTEC—The National Association to PROTECT Children
46 Haywood Street Suite 315
Ashville NC 28801
Phone (828) 350-9350 fax: (828) 350-9352
www.protect.org

Parents Anonymous Inc.
675 West Foothill Blvd. Suite 220
Claremont California 91711-3475
Phone (909) 621-6184
www.parentsanonymous@parentsanonymous.org

Childhelp USA
15757 N. 78th Street
Scottsdale, AZ 85260
Phone: (480) 922-8212
Toll-Free Hotline: 1-800-422-4453
www.childhelpusa.org/

The ChildTrauma Academy
5161 San Felipe, Suite 320
Houston, TX 77056
Phone: (713) 818-3967
www.childtrauma.org/

Child Welfare League of America
440 First Street NW, Suite 310
Washington, DC 20001-2085
Phone: (202) 638-2952
www.cwla.org/

Healthy Families America
Prevent Child Abuse America
200 S. Michigan Avenue, Suite 1700
Chicago, IL 60604
Phone: (312) 663-3520
www.healthyfamiliesamerica.org/

International Society for Prevention of Child Abuse and Neglect
25 W. 560 Geneva Rd., Suite L2C
Carol Stream, IL 60188
Phone: (630) 221-1311
www.ispcan.org/

Kempe Children's Center
1825 Marion Street
Denver, CO 80218
Phone: (303) 864-5300
www.kempecenter.org/

National Clearinghouse on Child Abuse and Neglect
330 C Street, SW
Washington, DC 20447
Toll-free: 1-800-394-3366
nccanch.acf.hhs.gov

National Data Archive on Child Abuse and Neglect
Surge 1 - FLDC
Cornell University
Ithaca, NY 14853
Phone: (607) 255-7799
www.ndacan.cornell.edu/

National Resource Center on Child Maltreatment
P.O. Box 441470
Aurora, CO 80044-2470
Phone: (303) 369-8008
www.gocwi.org/nrccm/

Tribal Court Clearinghouse: Child Abuse & Neglect
The Tribal Law & Policy Institute
8235 Santa Monica Blvd., Suite 211
West Hollywood, CA 90046
Phone: (323) 650-5467
www.tribal-institute.org/lists/child.htm

Know that you have the Courage to continue the Journey.

It has taken a Herculean amount of Courage to just remain here and — to the best of your ability — focused. Give yourself credit for being in this book, on this page, at this sentence, reading this word. All along the way you could have chosen to toss this book. You could have chosen to stop. But instead you have chosen to hang-in-there.

CONGRATULATIONS!

For you to even attempt this process takes Courage. It takes Courage to say to oneself: Perhaps the way I have been doing this is not the best way. It takes Courage to say to oneself: Um, I might have used too much force when I hit her. It takes Courage to say: Oh, My God!, I did hurt her. I did step across the line. I was abusive. My child was hurt by me. I *did* let him/her get hurt by someone else.

Feel God's Presence right where you sit. Take a deep breath. Each time you inhale, God's own Breath is breathing Life into each and every organ in your body. Each time you exhale, the Forgiveness of God is draining away, actually dissolving, every hurt of the past.

Go for it! Trust God. Believe in your ability to remain forthright, to remain truthful. Pray. Cry. But never give up. Don't stop until the Joy of God is your constant companion — *God's Promise.* You and your loved ones deserve the very best of you. God bless you. You can do this!

SEVEN

An Epilogue...

Of Promise

OUR time together, at this stage of our Journey, is over. It, has been a passage. And, I feel privileged, truly privileged, to have been chosen, by you, to act as teacher and guide, as you have traveled this Journey of Healing.

Healing, what a wonderful sacred word. It conjures up thoughts of God, Restoration, Grace, Peace, Jehovah, Christ, Truth, Infinite Power, Mind, Immanuel, Redemption, Atonement, Freedom, Wisdom, Goodness, Justice, Love, Joy, and Mercy.

For did we not find Her—Wisdom, accompanied by grace and Joy, as we have traveled this course?

Was not *Truth* a hair's breath away?

What did we seek, that we did not already possess?

Full circle, *this* is the road we have traveled together.—(what we experienced). We began our journey with a cry for help. Many of us feeling fragmented, disjointed, incomplete as in not whole. Damaged in some way. This, in actuality, was not true. *What God has put together, no man can put asunder.* And, now, through God's grace, we come to denouement, the unraveling, clarification; the solution—Seeing ourselves as is. Whole. Made, and *held closely* by our Creator, in the image and likeness of God. To be realized through one simple act. An act-of-faith. Faith in God.

Again, as stated before, when I use the term simple, I encourage you to keep in mind: "Simple but not easy."

God's solutions are most often unencumbered. Straightforward. Capable of being completed, in teeny tiny steps.

Your daughter died suddenly? Cry. Then wash your face and do what is in front of you to do.

Your child got kicked-out of school, with no chance of returning to *that* school, the one and only school you feel is good enough for him or her? Let the pain come through. Say: Oh My God! Pray. Ask for Direction. Then create a Plan-of-Action.

Your husband or wife been unfaithful to you? And, your gut is in wrenching pain and you are totally confused by this betrayal? Acknowledge the hurt. Say: Ouch! Tell God you are confused. Pray for the answer. And, wait. Wait for full clarity. Wait until you know that you know that you know, that God has given you the answer.

You have been diagnosed with an illness that you and or your family are afraid you are going to die from? Stand still with the reality of what is. Cry. Get mad. Seek God's solution. Recognize and acknowledge the power of God. Trust. And, believe. Believe that whether you live or die, each step you take, God will stay with you and be the Guide as well as your Comforter.

Are memories of hidden, and repulsed, and driven away abuse now a constant companion? Validate each memory. Acknowledge that it is real, that it did happen to you—let the pain surface. Cry. Call on God. Yell. Scream. And, get mad. Get mad at those who hurt you. Then nurture, soothe, and hold *you up* with esteem. And vow, with God's help, to take each and every step needed to heal.

Does the cutting, biting, anger-filled word and action seem like it has been with you forever? Have you screamed and hollered for so long it appears to be second nature to you now? Stand still. Face your behaviors head-on. Ask yourself: whose behavior have I been modeling? Acknowledge the shame and guilt that usually accompanies such awareness of grievous offenses on our part.

Call on God. Say: "God help me! Show me *Your* way. Grant me the grace to think, say, and do only that which *you* would have me think, say, and do." And then, Breathe.

Each suggestion offered is a simple straightforward way of handling a gut-wrenching situation. Easy? No. Absolutely, positively, not.

Those of us who believe in a power greater than ourselves frequently say: God didn't say it was going to be easy. What God said, *God's Promise*, was that He/She would always be with us and always supply our needs.

Spiritually grab hold of my hand. We've got one more stopover in our pilgrimage. One more stopover in our journey to a sacred place. That sacred place of promise—God's Promise.

Freedom

How do I let go of what I want—my image of what is or what, in my mind "should be"—and, embrace *what is*?

This question, I dare say, has been, pondered over by many folk, for years perhaps for centuries.

Those who have realized at least a modicum of the state-of-being that allows them to "let go and let God" tell us surrender is the key.

Oh oh; there's that word again. Surrender.

Earlier, in the book, we talked about some folk's view of surrender. In that, many think it is akin to waving the white flag of surrender. As in defeat, come and get me, I have failed, I am captured, some evil turmoil is now going to overcome me and take over. I am a failure. I am defeated.

However, those folk that I spoke to who have enjoyed the freedoms of surrender tell me to think, instead…

> Release.
> Let go—
> (as in opening my hands, palms facing
> upward and cupped, fingers spread wide).
> Liberate.
> Set free—
> as in setting free the problem
> as well as myself.

And, when I set free, liberate, that which is, a vacuum is realized—a space, to be filled (if I let it) by God. Filled—with God, God's Solution. Which has been germinating, smoldering under my heart, waiting for my embrace, and to ignite me with the fire-of-love—God's love.

Prayer

Heavenly Father & Mother, I call on you for help. I have been hurt. The pain is great. To the best of my ability I have acknowledged and opened up wounds. I have taken the recommended steps to heal those wounds. Where do I go now? How does this part of my Journey look? You have taught me that Life is a continuum. Just as with an onion, when it is peeled; as I unfold and look inside there is a layer, and a layer, and another layer, of me, that is revealed to me. Grant me the grace to: Breathe. Sit still. Be still. Hope. Wait. Believe.

Liberation:

Exercise:

Open your hands, with palms facing upward and cupped, your fingers spread wide. Extend your arms out in front of you lifting them slightly up and away from you. In your mind's eye picture one of the problems that you unearthed and worked on as we have traveled this Journey together. Place it in your cupped hands. As you extended your arms forward and up visualize yourself offering the problem to God. Say the following:

Into your loving care I place this problem. He/she did die. It hurt me so bad. I am powerless over the hatred I have felt toward You, me, him, and her. I can't do this any longer. Grant me the grace to let go. Grant me the grace to remember love. Grant me the grace to clean the slate; release the past; unbolt my grip on the pain and grief—the hatred of the past. Let me look at Now with eyes of mercy. Let me embrace what is with passion and gratitude.

Emancipation:

Exercise:

Sit for a moment with all of your (those) dreams deferred. Think about all of the self-imposed, sacrificial offerings—the constant insidious sacrifices made on your part. Let yourself feel the pain of a dream loss and the gut-twisting disappointment that comes from that. Embrace that pain—for, just a moment. Take a copious, rich, filled-with-meaning breath. A life-saving breath. Water your grief. Let the tears flow. Nourish, what was—your intention. Declaring: *Never more. Never more.* all the while praying as below:

I place the disappointments of my life into your loving hands Oh Lord. Heal your servant. What I had hoped for and envisioned, has been lost. Gone for all time. Bless me to let go of the person, the situation-the source of the anguish. Bless me to embrace *that which you have allowed to be. Everywhere I turn, in some form or fashion, you remind me of the gift of self, of the gift of me. I hardly believe it. But am willing to learn. Bless me to:*

- *Remember: There are others "out there" just like me-who have genuinely walked the walk and talked the talk and still the results of their efforts are, like mine — Barren.*
- *Remember: Each of your creations, all men and all women, have weaknesses — we each are fallible.*
- *Remember: To take "less personally" what has happened in my life.*

But most especially, Dear God, help me to remember that the way to peace and happiness is clemency.

Redemption:

Exercise:

Wait. That's right, wait. Whether you run around like a chicken with her head cut-off, or sit and wait, the betrayal that you experienced is still going to be real. There is a poem by Rainer Maria Rilke—Duino Elegies that talks about the "Value of Sorrow:" *Ah, we wasters of sorrow.* That's so true. Each second in our life, there is something to be gained.—Some type of enrichment to be experienced. So rather than try to run away from it, why not sit with what is, if but just for a moment? Visualize sitting on God's lap, resting your head on God's shoulder. Take a deep breath. Snuggle in real close. Comfy? Good. Now pray:

Heavenly Father, I call on you. Asking, that you grant me the grace to be willing to stay put, to remain here, in the here and now. Every breath that I take I am reminded of You, of the power in the moment: grace, joy and lessons to be learned. I ask for redemption, the kind that comes from release — releasing myself as well as the person I have held captive in that moment when they hurt me. I place my faith, my hope, and my Trust in You Oh Lord.

Restoration:

Exercise:

Take one of those cleansing breaths that rejuvenates each cell in your body. Put your arms around you as though you are hugging you for God. Smile. Listen. Listen to your breath; your heart beat; the sounds around you. Still your mind. And, keep breathing.

Now think on the following. Do you have: Cancer? Heart, kidney, liver disease? Lung damage? Bone, muscle or joint deterioration? Glaucoma, macular degeneration? Chronic and or acute pain?

Whatever the condition, embrace it. And, pray:

Dear God, you are both my father and my mother. And, I call on you. Knowing, in my heart, that you are with me. Pain and fear seem to be constant companions. Many times, I fear for my life and am scared about tomorrow. This isn't as I would have had it be. However, in faith, I release you and me from the bondage of hatred saying: Since you allowed it, I wouldn't have it any other way.

Grant me the grace:

> *To welcome what is*
> *To be as the sapling tree during a windstorm.*
> *Knowing, as it(the sapling) does*
> *that*
> *before, during, and after the storm —*
> > *You are there.*

I am being protected.
You are providing me with nourishment.
You are breathing peace and tranquility
into
the very marrow of my existence.

Deliverance:

Exercise:

Sit in a *(your)* safe place. If it is indoors, preferably a room with a window. Hum, quietly. Sway side-to-side, a bit. Rock, gently, ever so slightly as if barely moving while sitting in a rocking chair. If possible find a lush green tree. Look at it. Or place the image of a green in-full-bloom tree or plant in your mind. Breathing gently and rhythmically continue humming until you are centered in God. Pray:

I am your child. Bruised. Bloodied. Torn. Waiting, *for a healing. There was no reason for him, her, to have done* that *to me. I am still confused by what she, he, did to me. I hated you, me, and them. Now and again, asking: Why God? Why me? What happened was so horrible that I shielded, from its view, my eyes. But on today, I embrace it, knowing that this is the way to healing. And, I release you and me from the pinions of hatred. Step-by-step, breath-by-breath, embracing—you, me, activities of healing. Knowing, that like the Phoenix rising from the ashes — I too shall rise in glory.*

Absolution:

Exercise:

Think about someone you truly loved who is no longer with you. Think about the day they left you. Recall the moment you became aware, truly aware, that they would never again be in your life. Let the pain of that moment surface. And please, let the tears come and flow. Cry. Moan. Feel. Recalling that moment is an activity of pain. Let it hurt.

My friend, pain has a beginning and an end, so let it hurt.

As you are hurting, go one step further, allow yourself to remember the abusive behavior you have displayed toward another. Sit with the memory of the event(s) for just a moment. Embrace—unto yourself, validate, make real, take ownership of that which you did—(*not* "your intentions" but the <u>actual</u> behaviors displayed by you)—and then...Pray:

> *My God, My God, why hath Thou forsaken me?*
> *How, could you let me do that?*
> *Why didn't you stop me?*
> *This can't be true.*
> *I couldn't have done that.*
> *But alas, I did.*
> *Please God, I seek the healing balm..*
> *the elixir, of your loving mercy.*
> *Let me, as you have done, extend pardon to me.*
> *Let me walk in the Light-of-love.*
> *Let me know you.*
> *Let me feel the Presence of your love.*
> *Let me be free of yesterday.*
> *Let me embrace today.*
> *Let me heal.*
> *Let the chorus of the bird's song be present in my words.*
> *Let my touch be "pregnant" with softness.*

The spirit when properly fed, resides in a haven of forgiveness. Each prayer invites us into that haven.

Prayer, being present with God. Forgiveness, being present with God. Synonyms.

Someone, I can't recall who, once said something similar to this: *in essence, there is really nothing ever to forgive.*

We, each of us (even the rapist and the murderer), at any given moment in our lives (even at our worst moment) are doing, unfortunately, the very best that we can do.

Can we, and does God require us to, do better?

Yes.

It is up to us, our responsibility, to look for the love. To look for God's behavior, to look for *that* which God would do through us. And, then: Do it!

As I have traveled the course of my life, it has been a journey of inquiry, discovery, trial-and-error, gut wrenching failure and pain, betrayal—(me of God, others of me). It has been a NO DON'T LET THIS BE TRUE! IT CAN'T BE! walk.

And, it has also been: grace; cool breezes; healing; a loving touch; friends—genuinely concerned with my welfare—(putting socks on my bare feet in the dead of winter in Chicago Illinois as I catatonically walked about in the snow after someone's error in judgment that had caused me pain); healing cleansing tears running down my cheeks into my bosom watering my heart; a fortifying hug at my grandmother's funeral; money pressed into my hands, proffered, to feed my children, so I could remain in college; me finding roses placed on my hallway stairs in the dead-of-night to assuage my grief over the death of a loved one; me (in shock, by the iconoclastic turn of events) standing in a darken auditorium, shaking like a totally saturated deep, deep forest-green, wet leaf on a battered tree during a nighttime hurricane as I listen to my adult child's name called over-and-over as she is recognized for her gifts of intellect, compassion, sensitivity and the hope for tomorrow that she represented rather than the death (*her death — from drugs*) that I had prepared for.

Miracle. Each and every circumstance, a Miracle. From initial eye-opening at birth until final lids at rest *this* is what we are each graced to experience.

Most often, especially in my infancy of awareness, I failed to recognize that at, say for instance, the death of my grandmother I witnessed and experienced a miracle.

I did.

That is how she was able to "cross-over," and I was able to live through it.

Let's talk about this miracle for a moment.

Death, a Transition from one state-of-being to another. In that, the Spirit lifts up and out of its native soil (where it had resided sometimes for decades) and alights safely (finds haven) in that community of spirits-of-love.

Forgiveness is the passageway. It (forgiveness) is the active permit for me to enter this community of love.

Hatred and held-on-to grievances impede my egress. They stop myself from entering this glorious place, this league of love, the place where "the heart's immortal thirst to be completely known and all is forgiven," that Henry Van Dyke tells us about. As long as I am holding on to the pain and hurt of lifetime offenses, I can not enter that place.

It is impossible.

My hands are full.

Thereby stopping me from reaching out and embracing *that which is*. Now. My new home, my new birth, the next stop over in my Journey of love.

Authors abound, give us an inkling of the huge benefits of forgiveness:

Gerald Jampolsky M.D. — *Forgiveness – The Greatest Healer of* All

Dr Fred Luskin PhD — *Forgive for Good – A Proven Prescription for Health and Happiness*

M. Scott Peck M.D. — *The Road less Traveled-A New Psychology of Love, Traditional Values and Spiritual Growth*

Iyanla Vanzant — *Faith in the Valley*

Richard Carlson PhD. — *You Can Be Happy No Matter What* and *Handbook for the Soul*

Kent Nerburn — *Simple Truths: Clear and Gentle Guidance on the Big Issues in Life;*

Larry Dossey — *Healing Words* & journal *Alternative Therapies in Health and Medicine*

Pastor Robert DeGrandis S.S.J. — *To Forgive Is Divine*

The O (Oprah) Magazine September 2002 page 260 — *Does Prayer Work?* — about the inspiring life and work of Elisabeth Targ M.D.

Louise Hay — *You Can Heal Yourself*

Bernie Siegel M.D. — *Love, Medicine and Miracles*

Vincent P. Collins (booklet) — *Acceptance* — *The Way to Serenity and Peace of Mind*

Thich Nhat Hanh — *The Miracle of Mindfulness*

Bill Huebsch — *A Spirituality of Wholeness* — *The New Look at Grace*

Og Mandino — *The Greatest Salesman in the World*

Ernest Gaines — *A Lesson Before Dying*

Elisabeth Kuber-Ross M.D. — *On Death and Dying*

Maya Angelou — *I Know Why The Caged Bird Sings*

Peace Pilgrim — *Her Life and Work in Her Own Words* — Compiled by some of her Friends, Ocean Tree Book 1994

Trina Paulus — *Hope for the Flowers*

Margery Williams — *The Velveteen Rabbit*

The Holy Bible *King James Version. Cambridge, Cambridge.*
The Holy Bible *New Living Translation Wheaton IL.*
The Holy Bible *The New American Bible/The New Catholic Translation.* Nelson Publishing Company

The Torah

The Koran

The "Big Book" of Alcoholics Anonymous — *The Story of How Thousands of Men and Women Have Recovered from Alcoholism*

Elia Wise — *For Children Who Were Broken…For Adults Who Were Treated Badly As Children*

Foundation For Inner Peace — *A Course In Miracles*

Kenneth Wapnick PhD — *Christian Psychology in A Course In Miracles*

Al-Anon Family Groups — *Paths to Recovery — Al-Anon's Steps, Traditions, and Concepts*

Unity School of Christianity — *Consider The Lilies — Enjoying the Simple Life*

Alcoholics Anonymous World Services Inc. — *Twelve Steps and Twelve Traditions*

Janet Woititz — *Healing Your Sexual Self* and *The Struggle for Intimacy*

Ellen Bass and Laura Davis — *The Courage To Heal: A Guide For Women Survivors of Child Sexual Abuse*

Laura Davis — *The Courage To Heal: For Women and Men Survivors of Child Sexual Abuse*

Mike Lew — *Victims No Longer: Men Recovering from Incest and Other Child Abuse*

Melody Beattie — *Journey To The Heart* and other works

Wayne Muller — *Sabbath — Restoring the Sacred Rhythm of Rest* and *Legacy of the Heart — The Spiritual Advantages of a Painful Childhood*

Takeo Doi — *The Anatomy of Dependence*

Marsha Sinetar — *Do What You Want The Money Will Follow: Discovering Your Right Livelihood*

They each, in their own way, tell us to:

Release all that would stop us from embracing God.

Surrender.

Value self; *look* for the good.

Say, as Jesus did; *Peace I give to you, peace I leave with you. Father forgive them they know not what they do.*

Be the David as you create your own story rather than a victim.

Choose: always choose that which you will think, say and do: *that which you will embrace.*

Tap into and let flow freely from your heart the elixir so abundantly stored there by God—the sap of compassion, gentleness, tenderness, and caring.

Stand in the light, God's light of love, rather than the darkness of hatred.

See yourself as God does — A victor, a conqueror.

Live where God does — Now. We have a God of Now. Yesterday doesn't exist. Tomorrow is but a dream, a myth.

Look at you and me with eyes of mercy.

Remember, always, what Saint Paul so eloquently stated to the Romans centuries ago:

> *We are looked upon as sheep to be slaughtered. Yet, in all this we are more than conquerors because of him who has loved us. For I am certain that neither death nor life, neither angels nor principalities, neither the present nor the future, nor powers, neither height nor depth nor any other creature, will be able to separate us from the love of God that comes to us in Christ Jesus, our Lord.* (Romans 8: 36-39)

Goodbye my friend. And, may the peace that passes all understanding stand guard over your heart and mind in Christ Jesus.

ABOUT THE AUTHOR

SHIRLEY LUNDY-CONNOR is, by training, a behavioral scientist. Her field of study for the past 28 years has been to investigate systems of behavior—(both learning and social behavior)—and what effect, if any, environments especially depressed and impoverished environments have upon the developmental processes of persons.

This field of study led her to a master's degree in psychoeducational assessment and certification and licensing as an educational consultant.

To better serve persons within these environments she became licensed and/or certified in the areas of mental retardation, social maladjustment's, emotional disturbances, learning disabilities, and mild to moderate handicapping conditions-(kindergarten through 12th grade).

This work generated the development of an expertise that she uses as a mitigation specialist to: uncover evidence of significant contributory life trauma; develop multi-generational social histories; apply behavioral sciences theorem to the criminal justice process, especially capital cases; and, confirm or negate a possible correlation between participation in violent offenses and the absence of protective factors in families, schools, communities and peer groups.

Ms. Lundy-Connor acts as a consultant as well as presents broad and comprehensive trainings to social services agencies.

Participants in these trainings have included social workers, counselors, psychologist, psychiatrist, teachers, probation officers, lawyers, and therapeutic foster parents.

Ms. Lundy-Connor's skills as a clinician in the behavior sciences have been honed by:

- working in notorious inner-city public housing developments such as Cabrini Green in Chicago Illinois (where she began her career) and Desire/Florida in New Orleans Louisiana.

- acting as the assessment consultant on multidisciplinary evaluation teams, where she tests and then helps make determinations as to whether an individual is: mentally retarded; learning disabled; emotionally disturbed; behavior disordered; shows any signs of social maladjustment's; has any type of mild to moderate handicapping condition; or, is gifted.

- guiding, as director, the treatment design (which included individual, group, family, parenting, and incest survivors, therapy) of a nationally recognized residential drug and alcohol treatment facility for women and their dependent children.

She says what is of primary importance to her is: that her work be devotional; that she do her work as servant, as an act of faith, asking God's blessing on what she does; that she bring into God's Light her daily task for God's leading and healing; and, that she aspire to make all the moments of her day an offering of Love to God.

Ms. Lundy-Connor received the National Association of Social Workers Citizen of the Year Award in 1997 and The Spirit of Greatness Award in 1998. She is a member of the prestigious National Speakers Association where she is known as a powerful orator. Ms. Lundy-Connor's sincere commitment and ability to inform and inspire has earned her the reputation of being the speaker who galvanizes persons into action as she challenges them to (with God's Help) "Soar To Success!"

For information about additional books, tapes, workshops, retreats, and individual consultation sessions contact:

Shirley Lundy-Connor
Foundation For Living
P.O. Box 872631 New Orleans, LA 70187-2631
(504) 240-2114
recover@achieverecoverynow.com

www.ingramcontent.com/pod-product-compliance
Lightning Source LLC
Chambersburg PA
CBHW062042090426
42740CB00016B/2999